INTERNET OF THINGS

BOOK FOR THE TRENDING TECHNOLOGIES IN INTERNET OF THINGS

PROF. RAHENAAZ PATHAN

Copyright © Prof. Rahenaaz Pathan
All Rights Reserved.

This book is dedicated to those students and teachers who are willing to learn about the basic concept of Internet Of Things to create their own Hardware and Software applications about new Trends and Technology.

Contents

Foreword

If you want to learn any trend and technologies and you are willing to create any hardware and software application you need to clear your basic concepts of that particular domain. The Internet of things is useful to create many devices and connected applications. You can create different connecting applications using IoT concepts with different programming languages.

This book fully embraces the potential of the Internet of things to empower its users. It's a friendly and approachable text intended to help you level up not just your knowledge of IoT, but also reach your confidence as a developer for new trends in general. So dive in and get ready to learn - and welcome to the Internet of Things community.

- Prof. Rahenaaz Pathan

Preface

This book is for computer scientists,computer engineers and others who wants to learn and create better hardware and software applications using Internet of Things.

Our aim is to explain the enduring concepts underlying all computer system, and to show you the concrete ways that these ideas affect the correctness, performance, and utility of your application programs.This book is written from a devloper's perspective.

If you study and learn the concepts in this book, you will be on your way to becoming the rare "power developer" who knows how things work and how to fix them. Our aim is to present the fundamental concepts in ways that you will find useful right away. You will also be prepared to studying such topics as arduino, rasberry pi, and different sensors.

Acknowledgements

I would like to express my greatest appreciation to the all individuals who have helped and supported me throughout writing this book. I am thankful to my family members and my colleagues during this book writing for initial advice, and encouragement, which led to the final completion of the book.

I special acknowledgment goes to my motivators Mrs. Hetal Bhaidasna and Mrs. Kinnari Mishra who helped me in completing the book by exchanging interesting ideas and sharing their experience.

I would like to thank my special one who always motivated me to do my best in my career.

I wish to thank my parents as well for their undivided support and interest who inspired me and encouraged me to go my own way, without whom I would be unable to complete this book.

In the end, I want to thank my friends who displayed appreciation for my work and motivated me to continue my work.

- Prof. Rahenaaz Pathan

Prologue

In this book the basic details of Internet of Things is given and it is starting from the embedded system and about IoT advantages and Disadvantages as well as about architecture and Levels of IoT.

Before learning the concepts of IoT you aware about some basic Hardware and protocols as well as about some programming languages.

It has different versions can exist side by side. It is also Type safe and provides rich libraries of many built in functions.

Using Internet of Things you can create new trending smart systems.

I

Introduction to IoT

Embedded System:

Any electronic device's fundamental portion, or computer system, is known as an embedded system. These low-power devices are made up of a microcontroller or microprocessor embedded in an integrated circuit (IC) that performs a specific task.

An embedded system is the 'Thing' in the Internet of Things. In some ways, embedded systems are a subset of the Internet of Things. While the Internet of Things is a relatively new notion, embedded systems have existed since the dawn of the modern age.

Machine to Machine (M2M):

Machine-to-machine, or M2M, is a general term that refers to any technology that allows networked devices to exchange information and perform actions without the need for human involvement. Artificial intelligence (AI) and machine learning (ML) make it much easier for systems to communicate with one another and make their own decisions.

Machine-to-machine technology's main goal is to collect sensor data and communicate it to a network. Unlike SCADA or other remote monitoring tools, M2M systems frequently rely on public networks and access methods, such as cellular or Ethernet, to save expense.

Sensors, RFID, a Wi-Fi or cellular communications link, and autonomic computing software built to help a network device understand data and make choices are the primary components of an M2M system. The data is translated by these M2M apps, which can then activate preprogrammed, automated actions.

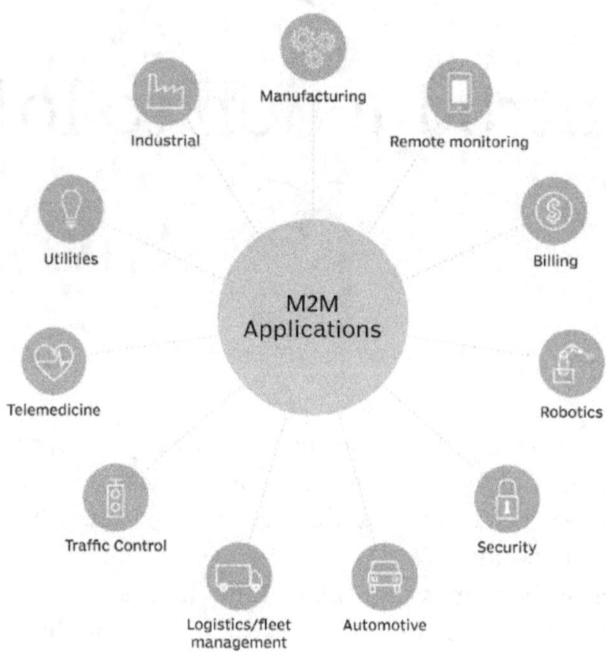

Machine to Machine (M2M) Applications

M2M system uses cellular or wired networks to transport data gathered from IoT-connected devices to gateways, the cloud, or middleware platforms, whereas IoT systems use IP-based networks to transfer data collected from IoT-connected devices to gateways, the cloud, or middleware platforms.

M2M	IoT
Machines	Sensors
Hardware-based	Software-based
Vertical applications	Horizontal applications
Deployed in a closed system	Connects to a larger network
Machines communicating with machines	Machines communicating with machines, humans with machines, machines with humans
Uses non-IP protocol	Uses IP protocols
Can use the cloud, but not required to	Uses the cloud
Machines use point-to-point communication, usually embedded in hardware	Devices use IP networks to communicate
Often one-way communication	Back and forth communication
Main purpose is to monitor and control	Multiple applications; multilevel communications
Operates via triggered responses based on an action	Can, but does not have to, operate on triggered responses
Limited integration options, devices must have complementary communication standards	Unlimited integration options, but requires software that manages communications/protocols
Structured data	Structured and unstructured data

Difference Between M2M and IoT

Definition of IoT:

The Internet of Things (IoT) describes the network of physical objects—"things"—that are embedded with sensors, software, and other technologies for the purpose of connecting and exchanging data with other devices and systems over the internet.

- **Definition of IoT based on existing technology:** IoT is a new revolution to the internet due to the advancement in sensor networks, mobile devices, wireless communication, networking and cloud technologies.
- **Definition of IoT based on infrastructure:**IoT is a dynamic global network infrastructure of physical and virtual objects having unique identities, which are embedded with software, sensors, actuators, electronic and network connectivity to facilitate intelligent applications

by collecting and exchanging data.

Characteristics of the Internet of Things:

There are the following characteristics of IoT as follows. Let's discuss it one by one.

1. Connectivity –
   Connectivity is an important requirement of the IoT infrastructure. Things of IoT should be connected to the IoT infrastructure.
2. Intelligence and Identity –
   The extraction of knowledge from the generated data is very important. For example, a sensor generates data, but that data will only be useful if it is interpreted properly. Each IoT device has a unique identity.
3. Scalability –
   The number of elements connected to the IoT zone is increasing day by day. Hence, an IoT setup should be capable of handling the massive expansion.
4. Dynamic and Self-Adapting (Complexity) –
   IoT devices should dynamically adapt themselves to the changing contexts and scenarios.
5. Architecture –
   IoT architecture cannot be homogeneous in nature. It should be hybrid, supporting different manufacturers ' products to function in the IoT network.
6. Safety –
   There is a danger of the sensitive personal details of the users getting compromised when all his/her devices are connected to the internet.

Application of IoT:

1. Smart Agriculture
2. Smart Vehicles
3. Smart Home
4. Smart Pollution Control

5. Smart Healthcare
6. Smart Cities
7. Smart Retail

Major component of IoT:

1. Things or Device
   These are fitted with sensors and actuators. Sensors collect data from the environment and give to gateway where as actuators performs the action (as directed after processing of data).
2. Gateway
   The sensors give data to Gateway and here some kind of pre-processing of data is even done. It also acts as a level of security for the network and for the transmitted data.
3. Cloud
   The data after being collected is uploaded to cloud. Cloud in simple terms is basically a set of servers connected to internet 24*7.
4. Analytics
   The data after being received in the cloud processing is done . Various algorithms are applied here for proper analysis of data (techniques like Machine Learning etc are even applied).
5. User Interface
   User end application where user can monitor or control the data.

3 layer rchitecture in IoT:

The physical parts, network technical design and configuration, operational methods, and data formats to be utilised are all specified in IoT architecture. IoT architecture can vary widely depending on how it is implemented; it must be adaptable enough to allow open protocols to accommodate a wide range of network applications.

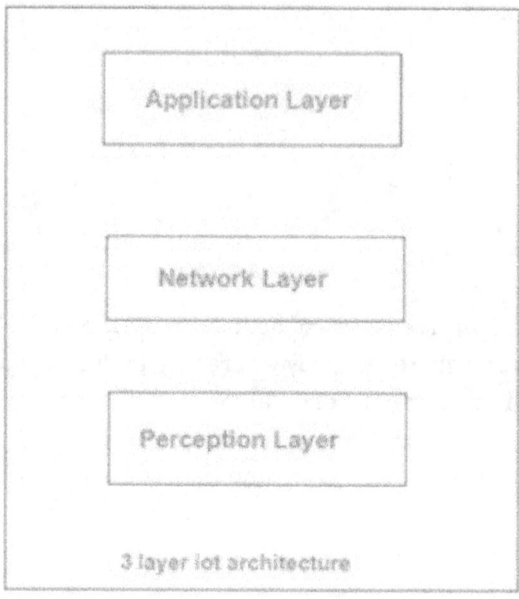

3 Layer IoT architecture

1. **Perception Layer** : The physical layer of the IoT architecture is this perception layer. Sensors and embedded systems are mostly utilized in these applications. Based on the needs, these capture large volumes of data. Edge devices, sensors, and actuators that communicate with the outside are included. It recognises specific geographical factors as well as other intelligent things/objects in the near area.

2. **Network Layer:** The data collected by these devices must be communicated and preserved. The network layer is responsible for this. It connects these smart/intelligent items to other smart/intelligent objects. In addition, it is in charge of data transport. The network layer is responsible for establishing connections between smart objects, network devices, and servers. It's also how sensor data is distributed and evaluated.

3. **Application Layer:** This application layer is where the user interacts. It is in charge of offering software resources to the consumer. For example, with a smart home app, users may turn on a coffee machine by pressing a button in the app. The application layer is in responsible of supplying

application-specific resources to the consumer. It defines several IoT applications, including smart homes, smart cities, and smart health.

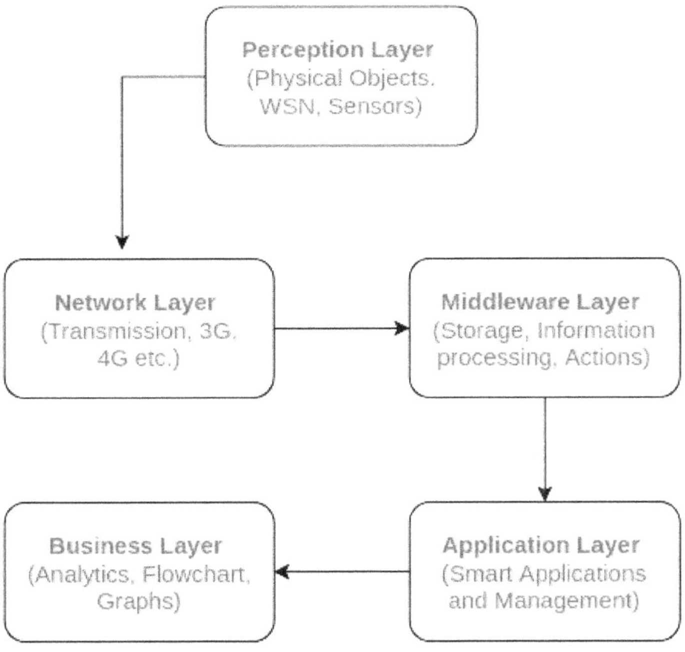

5 Layer Architecture

5 layer architecture in IoT:

1. **Perception Layer**: This is the first layer of IoT architecture. In the perception layer, number of sensors and actuators are used to gather useful information like temperature, moisture content, intruder detection, sounds, etc. The main function of this layer is to get information from surroundings and to pass data to another layer so that some actions can be done based on that information.

2. **Network Layer**: As the name suggests, it is the connecting layer between perception and middleware layer. It gets data from perception layer and passes data to middleware layer using networking technologies like 3G,

4G, UTMS, Wi-Fi, infrared, etc. This is also called communication layer because it is responsible for communication between perception and middleware layer. All the transfer of data done securely keeping the obtained data confidential.

3. **Middleware Layer** : Middleware Layer has some advanced features like storage, computation, processing, action taking capabilities. It stores all data-set and based on the device address and name it gives appropriate data to that device. It can also take decisions based on calculations done on data-set obtained from sensors.

4. **Application Layer:** The application layer manages all application process based on information obtained from middleware layer. This application involves sending emails, activating alarm, security system, turn on or off a device, smartwatch, smart agriculture, etc.

5. **Business Layer:** The success of any device does not depend only on technologies used in it but also how it is being delivered to its consumers. Business layer does these tasks for the device. It involves making flowcharts, graphs, analysis of results, and how device can be improved, etc.

IoT enabling Technologies:

IoT(internet of things) enabling technologies are:

1. Wireless Sensor Network
2. Cloud Computing
3. Big Data Analytics
4. Communications Protocols
5. Embedded System

Wireless Sensor Network:

A WSN comprises distributed devices with sensors which are used to monitor the environmental and physical conditions. A wireless sensor network consists of end nodes, routers and coordinators. End nodes have several sensors attached to them where the data is passed to a coordinator with the help of routers. The coordinator also acts as the gateway that connects WSN to the internet.

Example –

- Weather monitoring system
- Indoor air quality monitoring system
- Soil moisture monitoring system
- Surveillance system
- Health monitoring system

Cloud Computing :

It provides us the means by which we can access applications as utilities over the internet. Cloud means something which is present in remote locations.

With Cloud computing, users can access any resources from anywhere like databases, webservers, storage, any device, and any software over the internet.

Characteristics –

1. Broad network access
2. On demand self-services
3. Rapid scalability
4. Measured service
5. Pay-per-use

Big Data Analytics :

It refers to the method of studying massive volumes of data or big data. Collection of data whose volume, velocity or variety is simply too massive and tough to store, control, process and examine the data using traditional databases.

Big data is gathered from a variety of sources including social network videos, digital images, sensors and sales transaction records.

Several steps involved in analyzing big data –

1. Data cleaning
2. Munging
3. Processing
4. Visualization

Examples –

- Bank transactions
- Health and fitness data generated by IoT system such as a fitness band

Communications Protocols :
They are the backbone of IoT systems and enable network connectivity and linking to applications. Communication protocols allow devices to exchange data over the network. Multiple protocols often describe different aspects of a single communication. A group of protocols designed to work together is known as a protocol suite; when implemented in software they are a protocol stack.
They are used in-

1. Data encoding
2. Addressing schemes

Embedded Systems :
It is a combination of hardware and software used to perform special tasks.
It includes microcontroller and microprocessor memory, networking units (Ethernet Wi-Fi adapters), input output units (display keyword etc.) and storage devices (flash memory).
It collects the data and sends it to the internet.
Embedded systems used in
Examples –

1. Digital camera
2. DVD player, music player
3. Industrial robots
4. Wireless Routers etc.

Sensors:

A better term for a sensor is a transducer. A transducer is any physical device that converts one form of energy into another. So, in the case of a sensor, the transducer converts some physical phenomenon into an electrical impulse that determines the reading. A microphone is a sensor that takes vibrational energy (sound waves), and converts it to electrical energy in a useful way for other components in the system to correlate back to the original sound.

Actuators:

Another type of transducer that you will encounter in many IoT systems is an actuator. In simple terms, an actuator operates in the reverse direction of a sensor. It takes an electrical input and turns it into physical action. For instance, an electric motor, a hydraulic system, and a pneumatic system are all different types of actuators.

Controller:

In a typical IoT system, a sensor may collect information and route to a control center. There, previously defined logic dictates the decision. As a result, a corresponding command controls an actuator in response to that sensed input. Thus, sensors and actuators in IoT work together from opposite ends.

IoT Levels:

IoT level 1:

A level-1 IoT system has a single node/device that performs sensing and/or actuation, stores data, performs analysis and hosts the application.

Level-1 IoT systems are suitable for modeling low- cost and low-complexity solutions where the data involved is not big and the analysis requirements are not computationally intensive.

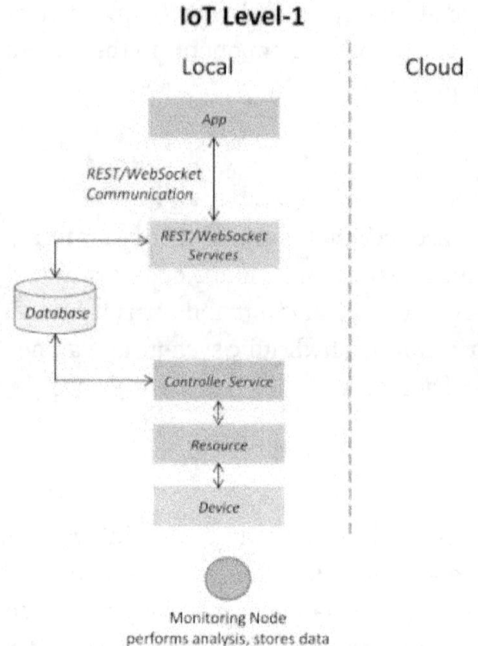

IoT level 1

IoT level 2:

A level-2 IoT system has a single node that performs sensing and/or actuation and local analysis.

Data is stored in the cloud and application is usually cloud- based.

Level-2 IoT systems are suitable for solutions where the data involved is big, however, the primary analysis requirement is not comptationally intensive and can be done locally itself.

IoT Level-2

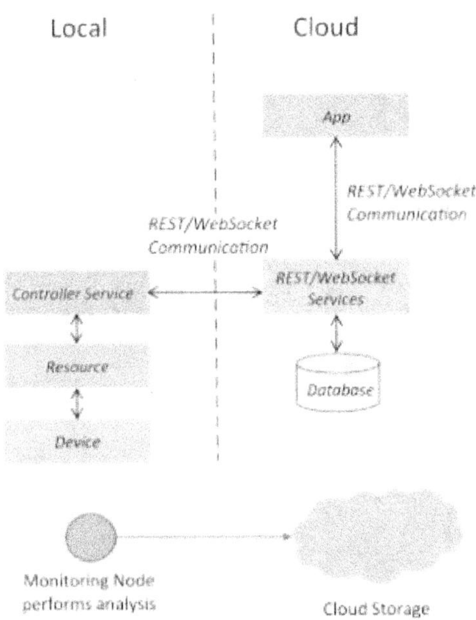

IoT level 2

IoT level 3:

A level-3 IoT system has a single node. Data is stored and analyzed in the cloud and application is cloud- based.

Level-3 IoT systems are suitable for solutions where the data involved is big and the analysis requirements are computationally intensive.

IoT Level-3

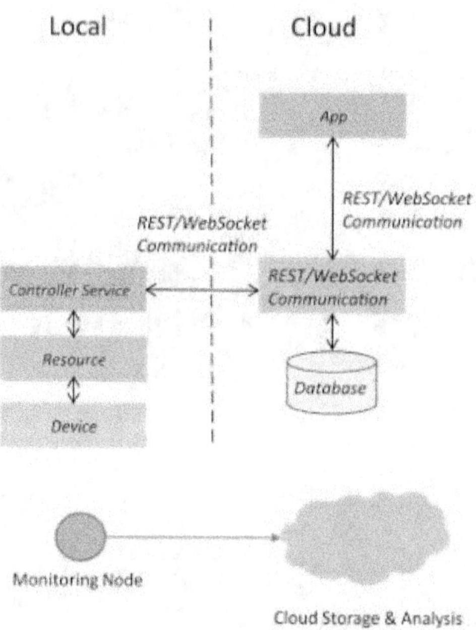

IoT level 3

IoT level 4:

A level-4 IoT system has multiple nodes that perform local analysis. Data is stored in the cloud and the application is cloud-based.

Level-4 contains local and cloud- based observer nodes which can subscribe to and receive information collected in the cloud from IoT devices.

Level-4 IoT systems are suitable for solutions where multiple nodes are required, the data involved is big and the analysis requirements are computationally intensive.

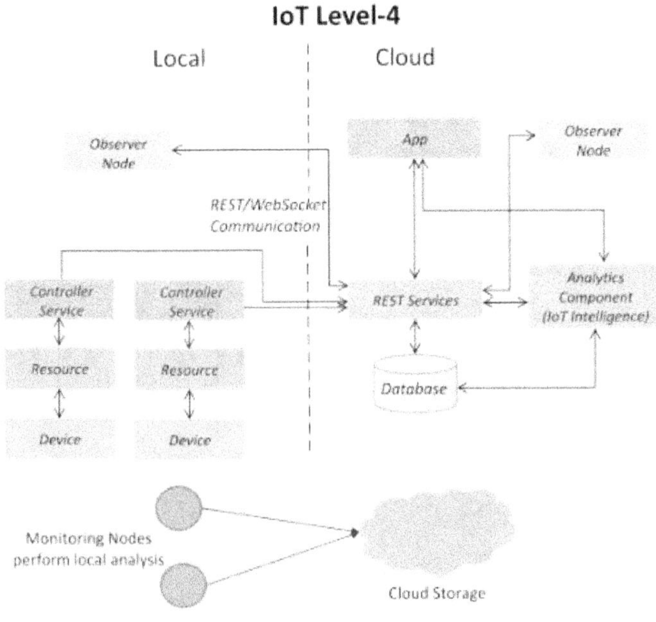

IoT level 4

IoT level 5:

A level-5 IoT system has multiple end nodes and one coordinator node.

The end nodes that perform sensing and/or actuation.

The coordinator node collects data from the end nodes and sends to the cloud.

Data is stored and analyzed in the cloud and application is cloud-based.

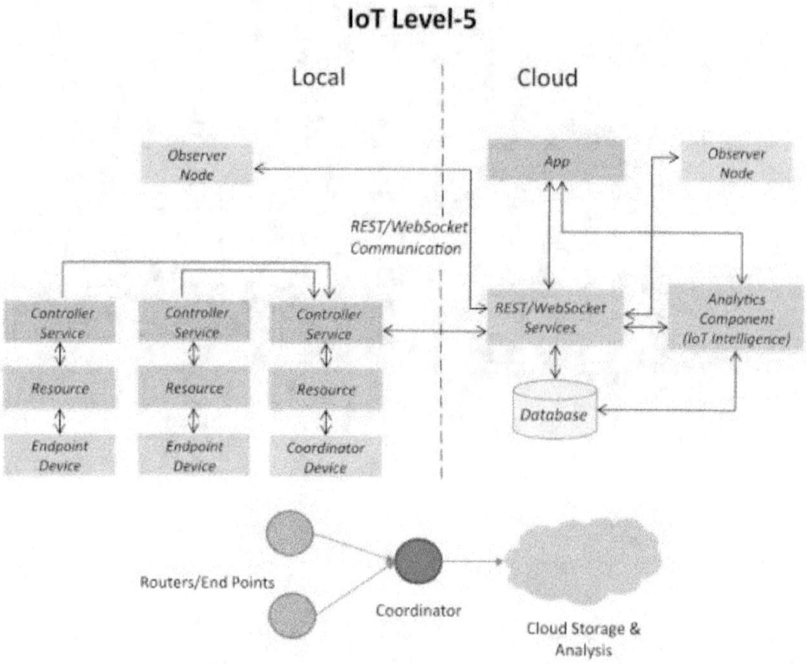

IoT Level-5

IoT level 5

IoT level 6:

A level-6 IoT system has multiple independent end nodes that perform sensing and/or actuation and send data to the cloud. The end nodes that perform sensing and/or actuation.

Data is stored in the cloud and application is cloud-based.

The analytics component analyzes the data and stores the results in the cloud database.

IoT Level-6

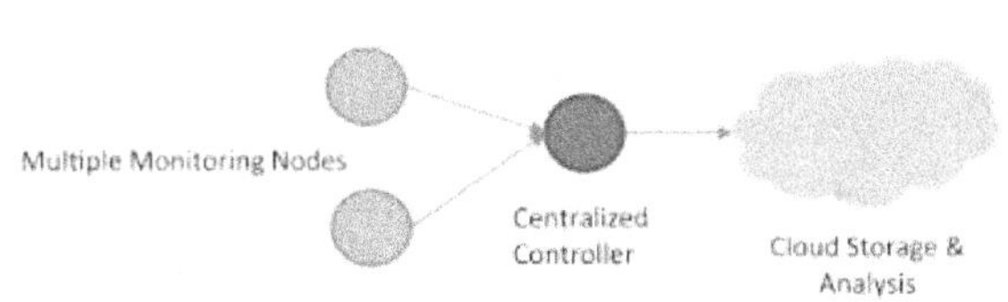

IoT level 6

II

Basic of IoT Networking

Zigbee:

ZigBee is a technological standard created for controlling and sensor the network. As we know that ZigBee is the Personal Area network of task group 4 so it is based on IEEE 802.15.4.

ZigBee is a standard that addresses the need of very low-cost implementation of Low power devices with Low data rate for short-range wireless communications.

Types of ZigBee Devices:

- Zigbee Coordinator Device – It communicates with routers. This device is used for connecting the devices.
- Zigbee Router – It is used for passing the data between devices.
- Zigbee End Device – It is the device that is going to be controlled

Zigbee Network Topologies:

- Star Topology (ZigBee Smart Energy)
- Mesh Topology (Self Healing Process)
- Tree Topology

Application of Zigbee:

- Simple remote control
- Medical applications
- Gaming
- Home automation
- Control and automation

Architecture of Zigbee:

Zigbee architecture is a combination of 6 layers.

1. Application Layer
2. Application Interface Layer
3. Security Layer
4. Network Layer
5. Medium Access Control Layer
6. Physical Layer

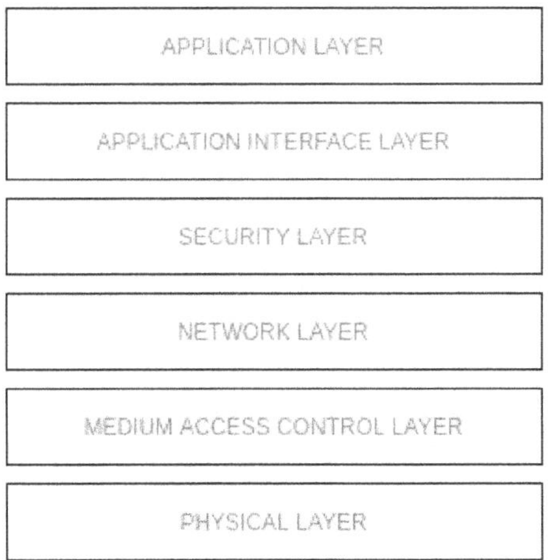

Zigbee Architecture

- The Application layer is present at the user level.
- The Application Interface Layer, Security Layer, and Network Layer are the Zigbee Alliance and they are used to store data and they use the stack.
- Medium Access control and the Physical layer are the IEEE 802.15.4 and they are hardware which are silicon means they accept only 0 and 1.

Channel Access:

1. **Contention-Based Method** (Carrier-Sense Multiple Access With Collision Avoidance Mechanism)
2. **Contention-Free Method** (Coordinator dedicates a specific time slot to each device (Guaranteed Time Slot (GTS)))

Zigbee Applications:

1. Home Automation
2. Medical Data Collection
3. Industrial Control Systems

Advantages of Zigbee Technology

1. High node support
2. Suitable for devices with low power
3. Range
4. Flexible
5. Monitoring

Disadvantages of Zigbee Technology

1. Channel noise:
2. The transmission rate is low
3. Security and compatibility
4. Expensive
5. Alternatives

Zwave:

Zwave is a protocol that is used for communication between devices for home automation. It allows low latency communication which is reliable of smaller data pack with data rate speed of 100kbit/second or 1GHZ. It uses for signaling and control and utilizes mesh topology that supports 232 nodes in a network with operating frequency of 908.42Mhz which differs in various country regions.It differs from the various country region. It uses GFSK Gaussian frequency-shift keying and there is control network controller devices set-up and manages Zwave network each logical Zwave has network home ID and multiple node IDS for the devices in it.

Application of Zwave :

1. Building automation
2. Remote control
3. Smart energy for home energy monitoring
4. Health care for medical and fitness monitoring
5. Home automation

RFID:

Radio Frequency Identification (RFID) is a method that is used to track or identify an object by radio transmission uses over the web. Data digitally encoded in an RFID tag which might be read by the reader. This is device work as a tag or label during which data read from tags that are stored in the database through the reader as compared to traditional barcodes and QR codes. It is often read outside the road of sight either passive or active RFID.

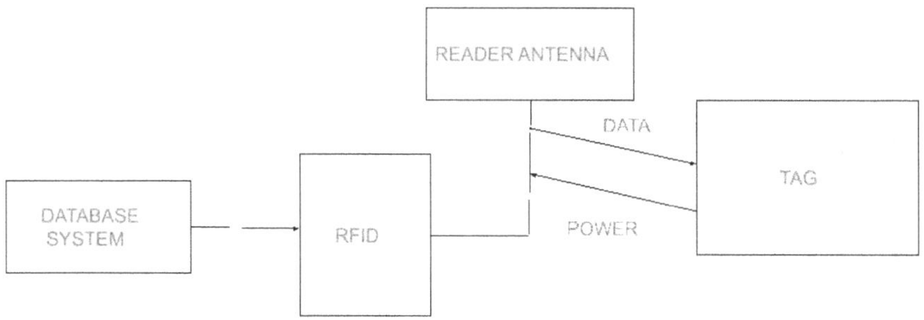

RFID

Kinds of RFID :

There are many kinds of RFID, each with different properties, but perhaps the most fascinating aspect of RFID technology is that most RFID tags have neither an electric plug nor a battery. Instead, all of the energy needed to operate them is supplied in the form of radio waves by RFID readers. This technology is called passive RFID to distinguish it from the(less common) active RFID in which there is a power source on the tag.

UHF RHID (Ultra-High Frequency RFID):

It is used on shipping pallets and some driver's licenses. Readers send signals in the 902-928 MHz band. Tags communicate at distances of several meters by changing the way they reflect the reader signals; the reader is able to pick up these reflections. This way of operating is called backscatter.

HF RFID (High-Frequency RFID):

It operates at 13.56 MHz and is likely to be in your passport, credit cards, books, and noncontact payment systems. HF RFID has a short-range, typically a meter or less because the physical mechanism is based on induction rather than backscatter.

There are also other forms of RFID using other frequencies, such as LF RFID(Low-Frequency RFID), which was developed before HF RFID and used for animal tracking

There are two types of RFID :

1. **Passive RFID –**

   In this device, RF tags are not attached by a power supply and passive RF tag stored their power. When it is emitted from active antennas and the RF tag are used specific frequency like 125-134MHZ as low frequency, 13.56MHZ as a high frequency and 856MHZ to 960MHZ as ultra-high frequency.

2. **Active RFID –**

   In this device, RF tags are attached by a power supply that emits a signal and there is an antenna which receives the data.

Working Principle of RFID :

Generally, RFID uses radio waves to perform AIDC function. AIDC stands for Automatic Identification and Data Capture technology which performs object identification and collection and mapping of the data.

An antenna is an device which converts power into radio waves which are used for communication between reader and tag. RFID readers retrieve the information from RFID tag which detects the tag and reads or writes the data into the tag. It may include one processor, package, storage and transmitter and receiver unit.

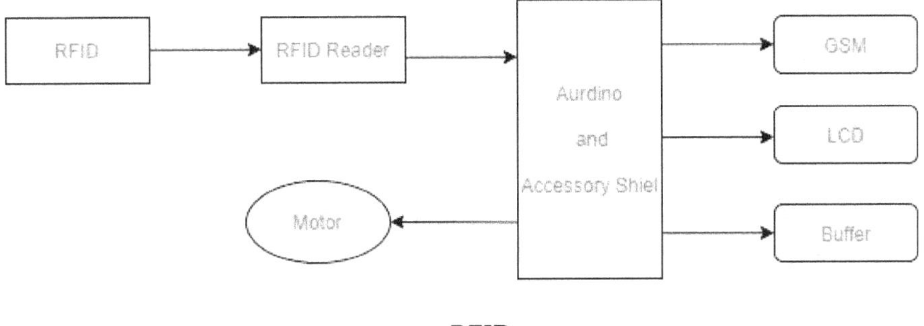

RFID

Features of RFID :

- An RFID tag consists of two-part which is an microcircuit and an antenna.
- This tag is covered by protective material which acts as a shield against the outer environment effect.
- This tag may active or passive in which we mainly and widely used passive RFID.

Application of RFID :

- It utilized in tracking shipping containers, trucks and railroad, cars.
- It uses in Asset tracking.
- It utilized in credit-card shaped for access application.
- It uses in Personnel tracking.
- Controlling access to restricted areas.
- It uses ID badging.
- Supply chain management.
- Counterfeit prevention (e.g., in the pharmaceutical industry)

Advantages of RFID :

- It provides data access and real-time information without taking to much time.
- RFID tags follow the instruction and store a large amount of information.
- The RFID system is non-line of sight nature of the technology.
- It improves the Efficiency, traceability of production.
- In RFID hundred of tags read in a short time.

Disadvantages of RFID :

- It takes longer to program RFID Devices.
- RFID intercepted easily even it is Encrypted.
- In an RFID system, there are two or three layers of ordinary household foil to dam the radio wave.
- There is privacy concern about RFID devices anybody can access information about anything.
- Active RFID can costlier due to battery.

NFC:

NFC stands for Near Field Communication. It enables short range communication between compatible devices. At least one transmitting device and another receiving device is needed to transmit the signal. Many devices can use the NFC standard and are considered either passive or active.

So NFC devices can be classified into 2 types:

1. **Passive NFC devices** – These include tags, and other small transmitters which can send information to other NFC devices without the need for a power source of their own. These devices don't really process any information sent from other sources, and can not connect to other passive components. These often take the form of interactive signs on walls or advertisements.

2. **Active NFC devices** – These devices are able to both the things i.e. send and receive data. They can communicate with each other as well as with passive devices. Smartphones the best example of active NFC device. Card readers in public transport and touch payment terminals are also good

examples of the technology.

How does NFC work? :

Like other wireless signals Bluetooth and WiFi, NFC works on the principle of sending information over radio waves. Near Field Communication is another standard for wireless data transition which means devices must adhere to certain specifications in order to communicate with each other properly. The technology used in NFC is based on older technology which is the RFID (Radio-frequency identification) that used electromagnetic induction in order to transmit information.

This creates one major difference between NFC and Bluetooth/WiFi. NFC can be used to induce electric currents within passive components rather than just send data. This means that their own power supply is not required by passive devices. Instead they can be powered by the electromagnetic field produced by an active NFC component when it comes into range. NFC technology unfortunately does not command enough inductance to charge our smartphones, but QI charging is based on the same principle.

The transmission frequency is 13.56 megahertz for data across NFC. Data can be sent at either 106, 212, or 424 kilobits per second which is quick enough for a range of data transfers like contact details to swapping pictures and music.

The NFC standard currently has three distinct modes of operation to determine what sort of information will be exchanged between devices.

1. The most common used in smartphones is the peer-to-peer mode. Exchange of various piece of information is allowed between 2 devices. In this mode both devices switch between active when sending data and passive when receiving.
2. The second mode i.e. read/write mode is a one-way data transmission. The active device, possibly your smartphone, links up with another device in order to read information from it. NFC advertisement tags use this mode.
3. The third mode of operation is card emulation. The NFC device can function as a smart or contactless credit card and make payments or tap into public transport systems.

Bluetooth:

It is a Wireless Personal Area Network (WPAN) technology and is used for exchanging data over smaller distances. This technology was invented by Ericson in 1994. It operates in the unlicensed, industrial, scientific and medical (ISM) band from 2.4 GHz to 2.485 GHz. Maximum devices that can be connected at the same time are 7. Bluetooth ranges up to 10 meters. It provides data rates up to 1 Mbps or 3 Mbps depending upon the version. The spreading technique that it uses is FHSS (Frequency-hopping spread spectrum). A Bluetooth network is called a piconet and a collection of interconnected piconets is called scatternet.

Bluetooth Architecture:

The architecture of Bluetooth defines two types of networks:

1. Piconet

2. Scatternet

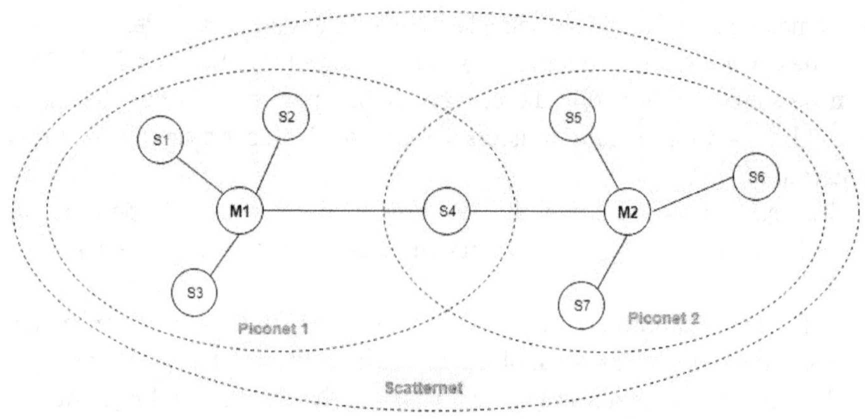

Bluetooth Architecture

Piconet:

Piconet is a type of Bluetooth network that contains one primary node called the master node and seven active secondary nodes called slave nodes. Thus, we can say that there is a total of 8 active nodes which are present at a distance of 10 meters. The communication between the primary and secondary nodes can be one-to-one or one-to-many. Possible communication is only between the master and slave; Slave-slave communication is not possible. It also has 255 parked nodes, these are secondary nodes and cannot take participation in communication unless it gets converted to the active state.

Scatternet:

It is formed by using various piconets. A slave that is present in one piconet can act as master or we can say primary in another piconet. This kind of node can receive a message from a master in one piconet and deliver the message to its slave in the other piconet where it is acting as a slave. This type of node is referred to as a bridge node. A station cannot be mastered in two piconets.

Advantage:

- Low cost.
- Easy to use.
- It can also penetrate through walls.
- It creates an Adhoc connection immediately without any wires.
- It is used for voice and data transfer.

Disadvantages:

- It can be hacked and hence, less secure.
- It has a slow data transfer rate: of 3 Mbps.
- It has a small range: 10 meters.

Applications:

- Used in laptops, and in wireless PCs.
- In printers.
- In wireless headsets.

Constrained Application Protocol (COAP):

The constrained application protocol is a client server-based protocol. With this protocol, the COAP packet can be shared between different client nodes which is commanded by the COAP server. The server is responsible to share the information depending upon its logic but has not to acknowledge. This is used with the applications which supports state transfer model.

Message Query Telemetry Transport (MQTT):

The message query telemetry transport protocol is a communication-based protocol which is used for IoT devices. This protocol is based on the publish-subscribe methodology in which clients receive the information through a broker only to the subscribed topic. Broker is a mediator which categorizes messages into labels before being delivered.

Secure Message Queue Telemetry Transport (SMQTT) :

SMQTT works as an extension to MQTT protocol. It is based on an encryption messaging mechanism that's why it provides a secure messaging standard. In this protocol, subscriber sends encrypted messages to all nodes and nodes receive encrypted message and use message after decryption. The encryption and decryption activities are carried out by using master key.

This protocol follows four main stages i.e., Setup, Encryption, Publish, Decryption.

0. In Setup, both publisher and subscriber register themselves near broker and get master keys.
1. In the Encryption stage, broker encrypts published message.
2. In the Published stage, broker gives encrypted data to subscribers.
3. In the Decryption stage which is last stage, data /message is decrypted by subscriber using that master key.

6LOWPAN:

The 6LoWPAN system is used for a variety of applications including wireless sensor networks. This form of wireless sensor network sends data as packets and using IPv6 - providing the basis for the name - IPv6 over Low power Wireless Personal Area Networks.

6LoWPAN provides a means of carrying packet data in the form of IPv6 over IEEE 802.15.4 and other networks. It provides end-to-end IPv6 and as such it is able to provide direct connectivity to a huge variety of networks including direct connectivity to the Internet.

With many low power wireless sensor networks and other forms of ad hoc wireless networks, it is necessary that any new wireless system or technology has a defined area which it addresses. While there are many forms of wireless networks including wireless sensor networks, 6LoWPAN addresses an area that is currently not addressed by any other system, i.e. that of using IP, and in particular IPv6 to carry the data.

The overall system is aimed at providing wireless internet connectivity at low data rates and with a low duty cycle. However there are many applications where 6LoWPAN is being used:

- **General Automation:** There are enormous opportunities for 6LoWPAN to be used in many different areas of automation.
- **Home automation:** There is a large market for home automation. By connecting using IPv6, it is possible to gain distinct advantages over other IoT systems. The Thread initiative has been set up to standardize on a protocol running over 6LoWPAN to enable home automation.
- **Smart Grid:** Smart grids enable smart meters and other devices to build a micro mesh network and they are able to send the data back to the grid operator's monitoring and billing system using the IPv6 backbone.
- **Industrial monitoring:** Automated factories and industrial plants provide a great opportunity for 6LoWPAN and using automation, can enable major savings to be made. The ability of 6LoWPAN to connect to the cloud opens up many different areas for data monitoring and analysis.

Wi-Fi:

Wi-Fi, in our mobile, laptop everywhere Wi-Fi is supported. Wi-Fi is a wireless networking technology, by which we can access networks or connect with other computers or mobile using a wireless medium. In Wi-Fi, data are transferred over radio frequencies in a circular range.

Wi-Fi, a brand name given by the Wi-Fi Alliance (formerly Wireless Ethernet Compatibility Alliance), is a generic term that refers to the communication standard for the wireless network which works as a Local Area Network to operate without using the cable and any types of wiring. It is known as WLAN. The communication standard is IEEE 802.11. Wi-Fi works using Physical Data Link Layer.

Nowadays in all mobile computing devices such as laptops, mobile phones, also digital cameras, smart TVs has the support of Wi-Fi. The Wi-Fi connection is established from the access point or base station to the client connection or any client-to-client connection within a specific range, the range depends on the router which provides the radio frequency through Wi-Fi. These frequencies operate on 2 types of bandwidth at present, 2.4 GHz and 5 GHz.

All the modern laptops and mobiles are capable of using both bandwidths, it depends on the Wi-Fi adapter which is inside the device to catch the Wi-Fi signal. 2.4 GHz is the default bandwidth supported by all the devices. 2.4 GHz can cover a big range of areas to spread the Wi-Fi signal but the frequency is low, so in simple words, the speed of the internet is less and 5 GHz bandwidth is for a lower range of area but the frequency is high so the speed is very high.

Let's say, if there is an internet connection of 60 MB/s bandwidth, then for 2.4 GHz bandwidth, it provides approx 30 to 45 MB/s of bandwidth connection and for 5 GHz bandwidth, it provides approx 50 to 57 MB/s bandwidth.

Applications of Wi-Fi :

- wirelessly.
- We can stream or cast audio or video wirelessly on any device using Wi-Fi for our entertainment.
- We can share files, data, etc between two or more computers or mobile phones using Wi-Fi, and the speed of the data transfer rate is also very high. Also, we can print any document using a Wi-Fi printer, this i**s very much used nowadays.**
- We can use Wi-Fi as HOTSPOTS also, it points Wireless Internet access for a particular range of area. Using Hotspot the owner of the main network connection can offer temporary network access to Wi-Fi-capable devices so that the users can use the network without knowing anything about the main network connection. Wi-Fi adapters are mainly spreading radio signals using the owner network connection to provide a hotspot.

Advantages of Wi-Fi

- It is a flexible network connection, no wiring complexities. Can be accessed from anywhere in the Wi-Fi range.
- It does not require regulatory approval for individual users.
- It is salable, can be expanded by using Wi-Fi Extenders.
- It can be set up in an easy and fast way. Just need to configure the SSID and Password.
- Security in a high in Wi-Fi network, its uses **WPA** encryption to encrypt radio signals.

- It is also lower in cost.
- It also can provide Hotspots.
- it supports roaming also.

Disadvantages of Wi-Fi

- Power consumption is high while using Wi-Fi in any device which has a battery, such as mobile, laptops, etc.
- Many times there may be some security problems happening even it has encryption. Such as many times has known devices become unknown to the router, Wi-Fi can be hacked also.
- Speed is slower than a direct cable connection.
- It has lower radiation like cell phones, so it can harm humans.
- Wi-Fi signals may be affected by climatic conditions like thunderstorms.
- Unauthorized access to Wi-Fi can happen because it does not have a firewall.
- To use Wi-Fi we need a router, which needs a power source, so at the time of power cut, we cannot access the internet.

Wireless Sensor Network (WSN):

Wireless Sensor Network (WSN) is an infrastructure-less wireless network that is deployed in a large number of wireless sensors in an ad-hoc manner that is used to monitor the system, physical or environmental conditions.

Sensor nodes are used in WSN with the onboard processor that manages and monitors the environment in a particular area. They are connected to the Base Station which acts as a processing unit in the WSN System.

Base Station in a WSN System is connected through the Internet to share data.

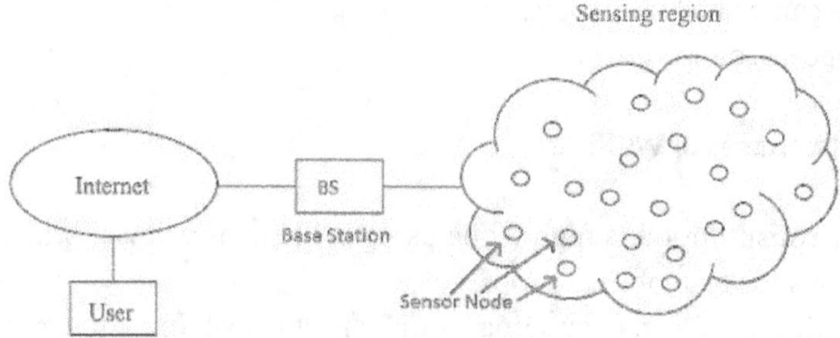

WSN

Applications of WSN:

1. Internet of Things (IOT)
2. Surveillance and Monitoring for security, threat detection
3. Environmental temperature, humidity, and air pressure
4. Noise Level of the surrounding
5. Medical applications like patient monitoring
6. Agriculture
7. Landslide Detection

Challenges of WSN:

1. Quality of Service
2. Security Issue
3. Energy Efficiency
4. Network Throughput
5. Performance
6. Ability to cope with node failure
7. Cross layer optimisation
8. Scalability to large scale of deployment

Components of WSN:

1. **Sensors:**
Sensors in WSN are used to capture the environmental variables and which is used for data acquisition. Sensor signals are converted into

electrical signals.

2. **Radio Nodes:**

   It is used to receive the data produced by the Sensors and sends it to the WLAN access point. It consists of a microcontroller, transceiver, external memory, and power source.

3. **WLAN Access Point:**

   It receives the data which is sent by the Radio nodes wirelessly, generally through the internet.

4. **Evaluation Software:**

   The data received by the WLAN Access Point is processed by a software called as Evaluation Software for presenting the report to the users for further processing of the data which can be used for processing, analysis, storage, and mining of the data.

III

Introduction to Arduino programming

Arduino:

Arduino is a project, open-source hardware, and software platform used to design and build electronic devices. It designs and manufactures microcontroller kits and single-board interfaces for building electronics projects.

The Arduino boards were initially created to help the students with the non-technical background.

The designs of Arduino boards use a variety of controllers and microprocessors.

The Arduino board consists of sets of analog and digital I/O (Input / Output) pins, which are further interfaced to breadboard, expansion boards, and other circuits. Such boards feature the model, Universal Serial Bus (USB), and serial communication interfaces, which are used for loading programs from the computers.Highest Salary in SQL

It also provides an IDE (Integrated Development Environment) project, which is based on the Processing Language to upload the code to the physical board.

The projects are authorized under the GPL and LGPL. The GPL is named as GNU General Public License. The licensed LGPL is named as GNU Lesser General Public License. It allows the use of Arduino boards, it's software distribution, and can be manufactured by anyone.

It is also available in the form of self practicing kits.

The Arduino is used for various purposes, such as:

- Finger button
- Button for motor activation
- Light as a sensors
- LED button
- Designing
- The Building of electronic devices

What is Arduino?

Arduino is a software as well as hardware platform that helps in making electronic projects. It is an open source platform and has a variety of controllers and microprocessors. There are various types of Arduino boards used for various purposes.

The Arduino is a single circuit board, which consists of different interfaces or parts. The board consists of the set of digital and analog pins that are used to connect various devices and components, which we want to use for the functioning of the electronic devices.

Most of the Arduino consists of 14 digital I/O pins.

The analog pins in Arduino are mostly useful for fine-grained control. The pins in the Arduino board are arranged in a specific pattern. The other devices on the Arduino board are USB port, small components, microcontroller, power connector, etc.

Features:

The features of Arduino are listed below:

- Arduino programming is a simplified version of C++, which makes the learning process easy.
- The Arduino IDE is used to control the functions of boards. It further sends the set of specifications to the microcontroller.
- Arduino does not need an extra board or piece to load new code.
- Arduino can read analog and digital input signals.
- The hardware and software platform is easy to use and implement.

History: The project began in the Interaction Design Institute in Ivrea, Italy. Under the supervision of Casey Reas and Massimo Banzi, the Hernando Bar in 2003 created the Wiring (a development platform). It was considered as the master thesis project at IDII. The Wiring platform includes the PCB (Printed Circuit Board). The PCB is operated with the ATmega168 Microcontroller.

Microcontroller : The most essential part of the Arduino is the Microcontroller, which is shown below:

- Microcontroller is small and low power computer. Most of the microcontrollers have a RAM (Random Access Memory), CPU (Central Processing Unit), and a memory storage like other computer systems.
- It has very small memory of 2KB (two Kilobytes). Due to less memory, some microcontrollers are capable of running only one program at a time.
- It is a single chip that includes memory, Input/Output (I/O) peripherals, and a processor.
- The GPIO (General Purpose Input Output) pins present on the chip help us to control other electronics or circuitry from the program.

Electronic devices around Us. We have many electronic devices around us. Most of the appliance consists of the microcontroller for its functioning. Let's discuss some of the examples.

- Microcontroller present in Microwave Oven accepts the user input and controls the magnet run that generate microwave rays to cook the food

and displays the output timer.
- Modern cars also contain dozens of microcontrollers working in tandem (one after another) to control functions like lighting, radio interface, etc.

Arduino Boards:

There are various Arduino boards that are used for various purposes. The board's I/O pins, size, and other characteristics vary. Microcontroller, Digital Input/Output pins, USB Interface and Connector, Analog Pins, Reset Button, Power Button, LEDs, Crystal Oscillator, and Voltage Regulator are among the components found on Microcontrollers. Depending on the type of board, some components may be different.

Popular Arduino boards.

- Arduino UNO
- Arduino Nano
- Arduino Mega
- Arduino Due
- Arduino Bluetooth

Shields:

Shields are hardware devices that can be put on top of a board to expand the project's capabilities.

The shield is as follows:

- When used in conjunction with Arduino, the shield can make projects much smarter and easier. Ethernet shields, for example, are used to link the Arduino board to the Internet.
- The shields attach and detach from the Arduino board with ease. It doesn't necessitate any complicated wiring.

What are the Arduino sensors?
Arduino is an open-source platform that allows you to create your own bespoke electronics projects. Let's start with a general understanding of sensors before moving on to Arduino Sensors.

What are the sensors?

A machine, module, or device that detects changes in the environment is referred to as a sensor. The sensors send a signal to the electronic equipment to inform them of the changes.

A sensor and electronic equipment are always in sync. Humans can easily read the output signal.

Sensors are now widely employed in everyday life. Controlling the lamp's brightness, for example, by touching its base, and so on. With new technology, the use of sensors is growing.

What is a sensor made of?

The sensor is a silicon device made up of single crystals. It is regarded as a common semiconductor material. It is more mechanically stable, machinable, and so forth. On the same substrate, it can also incorporate electronics and sensing devices.

Where are the sensors used?

The sensors are used to measure the physical quantities, such as pressure, temperature, sound, humidity, and light, etc.

An example of sensors is Fire Alarm, a detector present on the fire alarm detects the smoke or heat. The signal generated from the detector is sent to the alarming system, which produces an alert in the form of alarm.

The types of detectors are smoke detectors, heat detectors, carbon monoxide detectors, multi-sensors detectors, etc.

How are the sensors used in Arduino?

The data signal is sent from the sensor to the Arduino's output pins. The Arduino then records the information.

We'll go through several sensors in more detail later.

What are the types of sensors in Arduino?

Some of the types of sensors in Arduino are listed below:

○ **Light sensor**

The light sensor is used to control the light. It is used with LDR (Light Dependent Resistor) in Arduino.

○ **Ultrasonic sensor**

The ultrasonic sensor is used to determine the distance of the object using SONAR.

○ **Temperature sensor**

The temperature sensor is used to detect the temperature around it.

○ **Knock Sensor**

The knock sensor is used to pick the vibrations of the knocking. It is a common category of a vibration sensor.

○ **Object Detection Sensor**

It is used to detect the object by emitting infrared radiations, which are reflected or bounced back by that object.

○ **Tracking Sensor**

It allows the robots to follow a particular path specified by sensing the marking or lines on the surface.

○ **Metal Touch Sensor**

It is suitable for detecting the human touch.

○ **Water Level Sensor**

It is used to measure the water or the depth of the water level. It is also used to detect leaks in containers.

○ **Vibration Sensor**

The vibration sensor is used to measure the vibrations.

○ **Air Pressure sensor**

It is commonly related to meteorology, biomedical fields.

Arduino UNO:

The Arduino UNO is an Arduino standard board. UNO is an Italian word that signifies "one." The first release of Arduino software was given the designation UNO. It was also Arduino's first USB-connected board. It is regarded as a powerful board that is employed in a variety of tasks. The Arduino UNO board was created by Arduino.cc.

The ATmega328P microcontroller is used in the Arduino UNO. In comparison to other boards, such as the Arduino Mega board, it is simple to use. Digital and analogue input/output pins (I/O), shields, and other circuits make up the board.

The Arduino UNO includes 6 analog pin inputs, 14 digital pins, a USB connector, a power jack, and an ICSP (In-Circuit Serial Programming) header. It is programmed based on IDE, which stands for Integrated Development Environment. It can run on both online and offline platforms.

The components of Arduino UNO board are shown below:

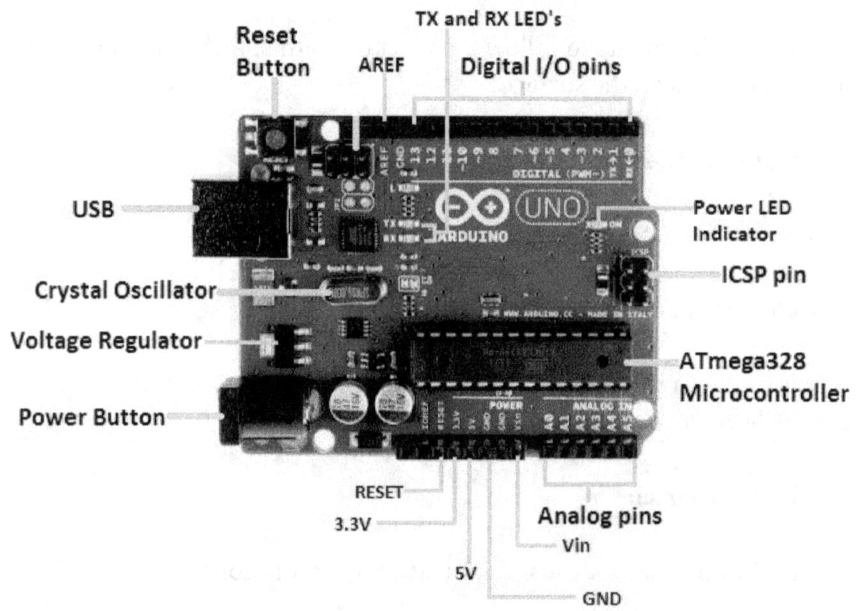

The components of Arduino UNO board

- The ATmel ATmega328 Microcontroller is a single-chip ATmel Microcontroller. It has an 8-bit processor code within. Memory (SRAM,

EEPROM, and Flash), an Analog to Digital Converter, SPI serial ports, I/O lines, registers, a timer, external and internal interrupts, and an oscillator are all included.

- ICSP pin - The In-Circuit Serial Programming pin allows the user to program using the firmware of the Arduino board.
- The ON status of the LED indicates that the power has been turned on. The LED will not light up if the power is turned off.
- Digital I/O pins- The digital pins have the value HIGH or LOW. The pins numbered from D0 to D13 are digital pins.
- LEDs for TX and RX- The lighting of these LEDs represents the successful flow of data.
- AREF- The Analog Reference (AREF) pin is used to feed a reference voltage to the Arduino UNO board from the external power supply.
- Reset button- It is used to add a Reset button to the connection.
- USB- It makes it possible for the board to communicate with the computer. It is required for the Arduino UNO board to be programmed.
- Crystal Oscillator- The Crystal oscillator has a frequency of 16MHz, which makes the Arduino UNO a powerful board.
- Voltage Regulator- The voltage regulator converts the input voltage to 5V.
- GND- Ground pins. The ground pin acts as a pin with zero voltage.
- Vin- It is the input voltage.
- Analog Pins- Analog pins are those with numbers ranging from A0 to A5. Analog pins are used to read the analogue sensor that is used in the connection. GPIO (General Purpose Input Output) pins can also be used.

Why is Arduino recommended over other boards for beginners?

The USB port in the Arduino board is used to connect the board to the computer using the USB cable. The cable acts as a serial port and as the power supply to interface the board. Such dual functioning makes it unique to recommend and easy to use for beginners.

What is the main difference between Arduino UNO and Arduino Nano?

The Arduino Nano has a compact size and mini USB cable than the Arduino UNO.

What is the main difference between Arduino UNO and Arduino Mega?

The Arduino UNO is a standard board recommended to beginners, while Arduino Mega is used for complex projects due to its greater memory space.

Memory:

The memory structure is shown in the below image:

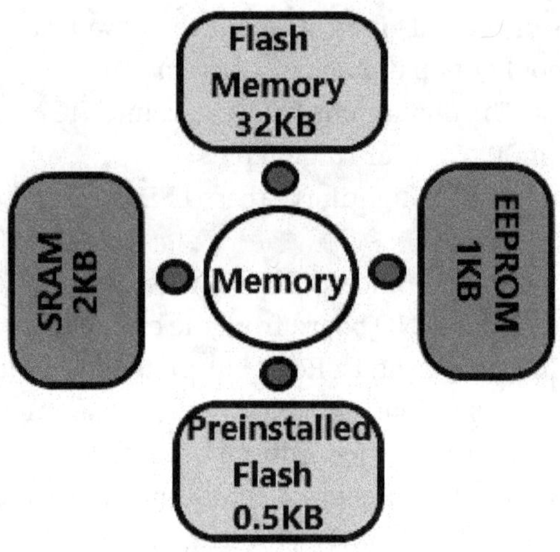

Memory

The preinstalled flash has a bootloader, which takes the memory of 0.5 Kb.

Here, SRAM stands for Static Random Access Memory, and EEPROM stands for Electrically Erasable Programmable Read-Only Memory.

Technical Specifications of Arduino UNO:

The technical specifications of the Arduino UNO are listed below:

- There are 20 Input/Output pins present on the Arduino UNO board. These 20 pis include 6 PWM pins, 6 analog pins, and 8 digital I/O pins.
- The PWM pins are Pulse Width Modulation capable pins.
- The crystal oscillator present in Arduino UNO comes with a frequency of 16MHz.
- It also has an Arduino WiFi module built in. The Integrated WiFi ESP8266 Module and the ATmega328P microprocessor are used in this Arduino UNO board.
- The UNO board's input voltage ranges from 7 to 20 volts.

- The Arduino UNO is powered by an external power supply by default. It can also get power via a USB port.

How to get started with Arduino UNO?

We can program the Arduino UNO using the Arduino IDE. The Arduino IDE is the Integral Development program, which is common to all the boards.

We can also use Arduino Web Editor, which allows us to upload sketches and write the code from our web browser (Google Chrome recommended) to any Arduino Board. It is an online platform.

The USB connection is essential to connect the computer with the board. After the connection, the PWR pins will be light green. It is a green power LED.

The steps to get started with Arduino UNO are listed below:

- Install the **drivers** of the board.

As soon we connect the board to the computer, Windows from XP to 10 will automatically install the board drivers. But, if you have expanded or downloaded the zip package, follow the below steps:

1. Click on **Start** --> **Control Panel** --> **System and Security**.
2. Click on **System** --> **Device Manager** --> **Ports (COM &LPT)** --> **Arduino UNO**. If the COM &LPT is absent, look **Other Devices** --> **Unknown Device.**
3. Right-click to **Arduino UNO** --> **Update Driver Software** --> **Browse my computer for driver software.**
4. Select the file "**inf**" to navigate else, select "**ArduinoUNO.inf**".
5. Installation Finished.

- Open the code or sketch written in the Arduino software.
- Select the type of board.
  Click on **'Tools'** and select **Board**, as shown below:

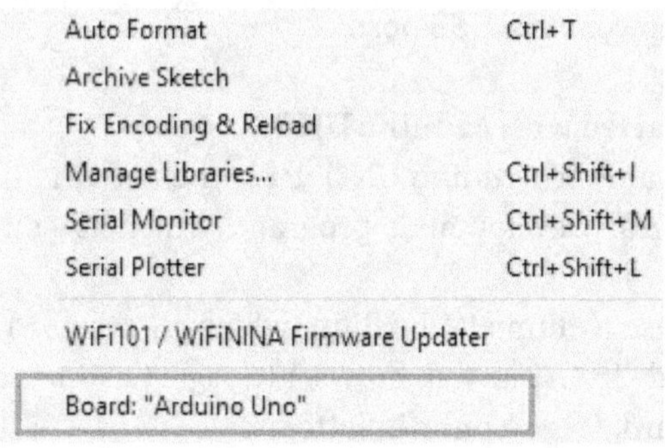

- Select the port. Click on the **Tools -> Port** (select the port). The port likely will be **COM3** or higher. For example, **COM6**, etc. The **COM1** and **COM2** ports will not appear, because these two ports are reserved for the hardware serial ports.
- Now, **upload** and **run** the written code or sketch.

To upload and run, click on the button present on the top panel of the Arduino display, as shown below:

Within the few seconds after the compile and run of code or sketch, the RX and TX light present on the Arduino board will flash.

The 'Done Uploading' message will appear after the code is successfully uploaded. The message will be visible in the status bar.

Arduino Coding Basics

We have already discussed the popular Arduino Boards, Arduino IDEs, and the Installation process of the Arduino software. We learned that Arduino IDE (Integrated Development Environment) allows us to draw the sketch and upload it to the various Arduino Boards using code. The code is written in a simple programming language similar to C and C++.

The initial step to start with Arduino is the IDE download and installation.

Let's discuss the basics to start with Arduino programming.

Brackets

There are two types of brackets used in the Arduino coding, which are listed below:

- Parentheses ( )
- Curly Brackets { }

Parentheses ( )

The parentheses brackets are the group of the arguments, such as method, function, or a code statement. These are also used to group the math equations.

Curly Brackets { }

The statements in the code are enclosed in curly brackets. We always require closed curly brackets to match the open curly bracket in the code or sketch.

Open curly bracket- ' { '

Closed curly bracket - ' } '

Line Comment

There are two types of line comments, which are listed below:

- Single line comment
- Multi-line comment

// Single line comment

The text that is written after the two forward slashes are considered as a single line comment. The compiler ignores the code written after the two forward slashes. The comment will not be displayed in the output. Such text is specified for a better understanding of the code or for the explanation of any code statement.

The // (two forward slashes) are also used to ignore some extra lines of code without deleting it.

/* Multi - line comment */

The Multi-line comment is written to group the information for clear understanding. It starts with the single forward slash and an asterisk symbol (/ *). It also ends with the / *. It is commonly used to write the larger text. It is a comment, which is also ignored by the compiler.

Coding Screen

The coding screen is divided into two blocks. The setup is considered as the preparation block, while the loop is considered as the execution block. It is shown below:

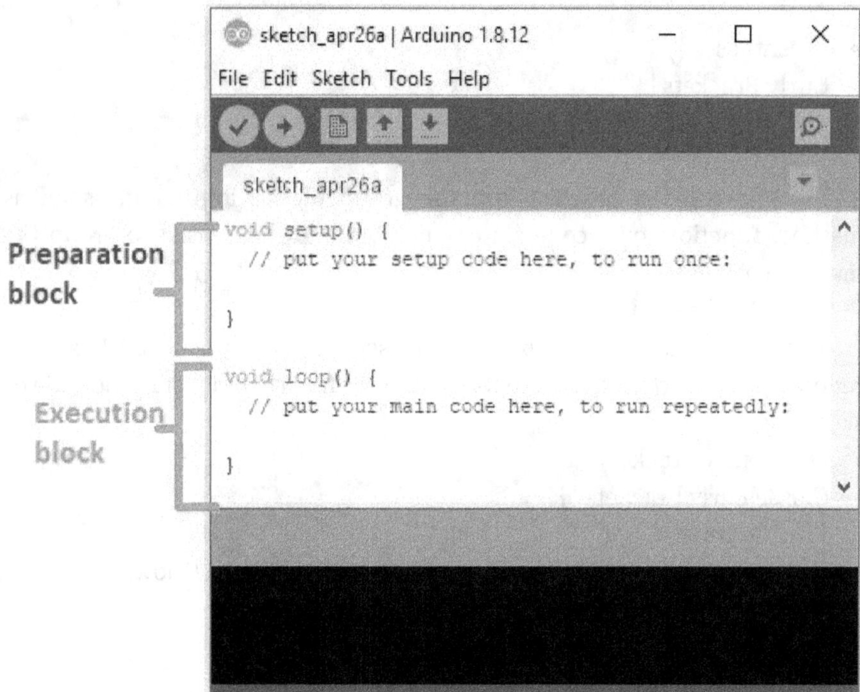

The set of statements in the setup and loop blocks are enclosed with the curly brackets. We can write multiple statements depending on the coding requirements for a particular project.

For example:

void setup ( )
{
Coding statement 1;
Coding statement 2;
Coding statement n;
}
void loop ( )

```
{
Coding statement 1;
Coding statement 2;
Coding statement n;
}
```

What is Setup? What type of code is written in the setup block?

It contains an initial part of the code to be executed. The pin modes, libraries, variables, etc., are initialized in the setup section. It is executed only once during the uploading of the program and after reset or power up of the Arduino board.

Zero setup () resides at the top of each sketch. As soon as the program starts running, the code inside the curly bracket is executed in the setup and it executes only once.

What is Loop? What type of code is written in the Loop block?

The loop contains statements that are executed repeatedly. The section of code inside the curly brackets is repeated depending on the value of variables.

Time in Arduino

The time in Arduino programming is measured in a millisecond.

Where, 1 sec = 1000 milliseconds

We can adjust the timing according to the milliseconds.

For example, for a 5-second delay, the time displayed will be 5000 milliseconds.

Example:

Let's consider a simple LED blink example.

The steps to open such example are:

1. Click on the File button, which is present on the menu bar.
2. Click on the Examples.
3. Click on the Basics option and click on the Blink

The example will reopen in a new window, as shown below:

```
Blink                                              ▼

void setup() {                                      ^
    // initialize digital pin LED_BUILTIN as an outpu'
    pinMode(LED_BUILTIN, OUTPUT);
}


// the loop function runs over and over again forev
void loop() {
    digitalWrite(LED_BUILTIN, HIGH);    // turn the LEI
    delay(1000);                        // wait for a
    digitalWrite(LED_BUILTIN, LOW);     // turn the LEI
    delay(1000);                        // wait for a  ∨
<                                                   >
```

- The void setup () would include pinMode as the main function.

pinMode ( )

The specific pin number is set as the INPUT or OUTPUT in the pinMode () function.

The Syntax is: **pinMode (pin, mode)**

Where,

pin: It is the pin number. We can select the pin number according to the requirements.

Mode: We can set the mode as INPUT or OUTPUT according to the corresponding pin number.

Let' understand the pinMode with an example.

Example: We want to set the 12 pin number as the output pin.

Code:

1. pinMode (12, OUTPUT);

Why is it recommended to set the mode of pins as OUTPUT?

The OUTPUT mode of a specific pin number provides a considerable amount of current to other circuits, which is enough to run a sensor or to light the LED brightly. The output state of a pin is considered as the low-impedance state.

The high current and short circuit of a pin can damage the ATmel chip. So, it is recommended to set the mode as OUTPUT.

Can we set the pinMode as INPUT?

The digitalWrite () will disable the LOW during the INPUT mode. The output pin will be considered as HIGH.

We can use the INPUT mode to use the external pull-down resistor. We are required to set the pinMode as INPUT_PULLUP. It is used to reverse the nature of the INPUT mode.

The sufficient amount of current is provided by the pull-up mode to dimly light an LED, which is connected to the pin in the INPUT mode. If the LED is working dimly, it means this condition is working out.

Due to this, it is recommended to set the pin in OUTPUT mode.

○ The void loop () would include **digitalWrite( )** and **delay ( )** as the main function.

digitalWrite( )

The digitalWrite ( ) function is used to set the value of a pin as HIGH or LOW.

Where,

HIGH: It sets the value of the voltage. For the 5V board, it will set the value of 5V, while for 3.3V, it will set the value of 3.3V.

LOW: It sets the value = 0 (GND).

If we do not set the pinMode as OUTPUT, the LED may light dim.

The syntax is: **digitalWrite(pin, value HIGH/LOW)**

pin: We can specify the pin number or the declared variable.

Let's understand with an example.

Example:

1. digitalWrite (13, HIGH);
2. digitalWrite (13, LOW);

The HIGH will ON the LED and LOW will OFF the LED connected to pin number 13.

What is the difference between digitalRead () and digitalWrite ()?

The digitalRead () function will read the HIGH/LOW value from the digital pin, and the digitalWrite () function is used to set the HIGH/LOW value of the digital pin.

delay ( )

The delay () function is a blocking function to pause a program from doing a task during the specified duration in milliseconds.

For example, - delay (2000)

Where, 1 sec = 1000millisecond

Hence, it will provide a delay of 2 seconds.

Code:

1. digitalWrite (13, HIGH);
2. delay (2000);
3. digitalWrite (13, LOW);
4. delay (1000);

Here, the LED connected to pin number 13 will be ON for 2 seconds and OFF for 1 second. The task will repeatedly execute as it is in the void loop ().

We can set the duration according to our choice or project requirements.

Example: To light the LED connected to pin number 13. We want to ON the LED for 4 seconds and OFF the LED for 1.5 seconds.

Code:

```
void setup ()
{
pinMode ( 13, OUTPUT); // to set the OUTPUT mode of pin number 13.
}
void loop ()
{
digitalWrite (13, HIGH);
delay (4000); // 4 seconds = 4 x 1000 milliseconds
digitalWrite (13, LOW);
delay (1500); // 1.5 seconds = 1.5 x 1000 milliseconds
}
```

Arduino Syntax and Program Flow

Syntax

Syntax in Arduino signifies the rules that need to be followed for the successful uploading of the Arduino program to the board. The syntax of

Arduino is similar to the grammar in English. It means that the rules must be followed in order to compile and run our code successfully. If we break those rules, our computer program may compile and run, but with some bugs.

Let's understand with an example.

As we open the Arduino IDE, the display will look like the below image:

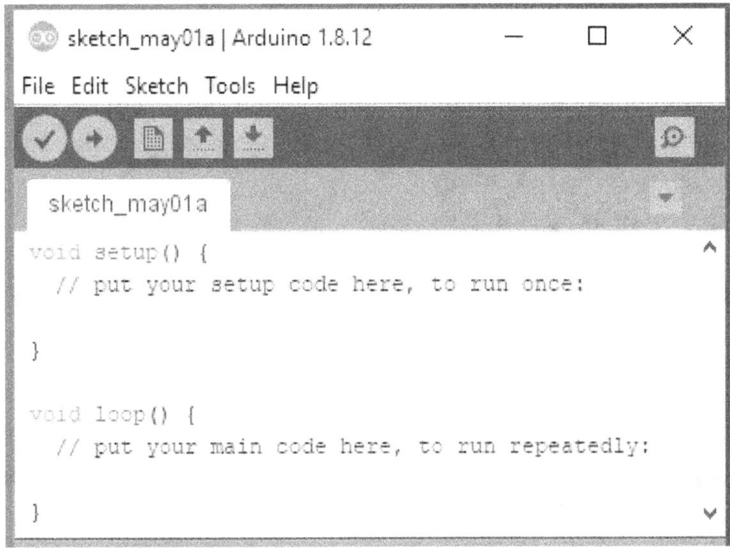

The two functions that encapsulate the pieces of code in the Arduino program are shown below:

1. **void setup ( )**
2. **void loop ( )**

Functions

- The functions in Arduino combine many pieces of lines of code into one.
- The functions usually return a value after finishing execution. But here, the function does not return any value due to the presence of void.
- The setup and loop function have **void** keyword present in front of their function name.

- The multiple lines of code that a function encapsulates are written inside curly brackets.
- Every closing curly bracket ' } ' must match the opening curly bracket '{ ' in the code.
- We can also write our own functions, which will be discussed later in this tutorial.

Spaces

- Arduino ignores the white spaces and tabs before the coding statements.
- The coding statements in the code are intent (empty spacing at the starting) for the easy reading.
- In the function definition, loop, and conditional statements, 1 intent = 2 spaces.
- The compiler of Arduino also ignores the spaces in the parentheses, commas, blank lines, etc.

Tools Tab

- The verify icon present on the tool tab only compiles the code. It is a quick method to check that whether the syntax of our program is correct or not.
- To compile, run, and upload the code to the board, we need to click on the Upload button.

Uses of Parentheses ( )

- It denotes the function like void setup ( ) and void loop ( ).
- The parameter's inputs to the function are enclosed within the parentheses.
- It is also used to change the order of operations in mathematical operations.

Semicolon ;

- It is the statement terminator in the C as well as C++.
- A statement is a command given to the Arduino, which instructs it to take some kind of action. Hence, the terminator is essential to signify the

end of a statement.

- We can write one or more statements in a single line, but with semicolon indicating the end of each statement.
- The compiler will indicate an error if a semicolon is absent in any of the statements.
- It is recommended to write each statement with semicolon in a different line, which makes the code easier to read.
- We are not required to place a semicolon after the curly braces of the setup and loop function.

Arduino processes each statement sequentially. It executes one statement at a time before moving to the next statement.

Program Flow

The program flow in Arduino is similar to the flowcharts. It represents the execution of a program in order.

We recommend to draw the flowchart before writing the code. It helps us to understand the concept of code, which makes it the coding simpler and easier.

Flow Charts

A flowchart uses shapes and arrows to represent the information or sequence of actions.

An oval ellipse shows the Start of the sequence, and a square shows the action or processes that need to be performed.

The Arduino coding process in the form of the flowchart is shown below:

Setup ( ): **Acts as an entry point**

Here, the processor enters our code, and the execution of code begins. After the setup, the execution of the statement in the loop begins.

loop ( ) : **runs over and over again**

The example of the flowchart in Arduino is shown below:

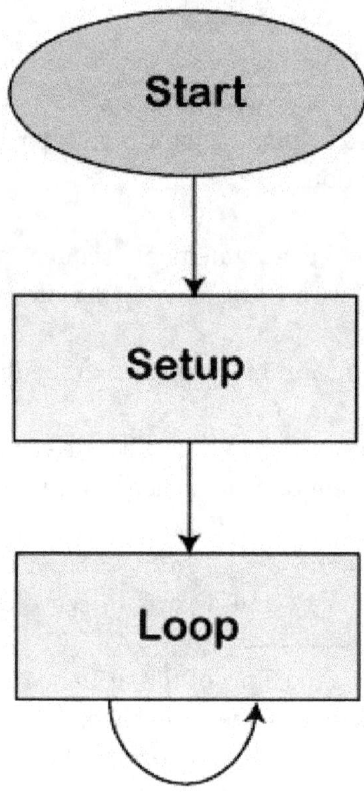

Flow chart of Arduino

NodeMCU:

NodeMCU is an open-source LUA based firmware developed for the ESP8266 wifi chip. By exploring functionality with the ESP8266 chip, NodeMCU firmware comes with the ESP8266 Development board/kit i.e. NodeMCU Development board.

NodeMCU Development Board/kit v0.9 (Version1)

Since NodeMCU is an open-source platform, anyone can edit, tweak, or manufacture its hardware.

The ESP8266 wifi-enabled chip is used in the NodeMCU Dev Kit/board. The ESP8266 is a low-cost Wi-Fi chip with TCP/IP protocol designed by Espressif Systems. The ESP8266 WiFi Module has more information about the ESP8266.

Version 2 (V2) of the NodeMCU Dev Kit is available, namely NodeMCU Development Board v1.0 (Version2), which is typically black in color.

NodeMCU Development Board/kit v1.0 (Version2)

For more information about NodeMCU Boards available in the market refer to NodeMCU development boards.

NodeMCU Dev Kit has Arduino like Analog (i.e. A0) and Digital (D0-D8) pins on its board.

It supports serial communication protocols i.e. UART, SPI, I2C, etc.

Using such serial protocols we can connect it with serial devices like I2C enabled LCD display, Magnetometer HMC5883, MPU-6050 Gyro meter + Accelerometer, RTC chips, GPS modules, touch screen displays, SD cards, etc.

How to start with NodeMCU?

Wifi functionality, analogue pins, digital pins, and serial communication protocols are all included on the NodeMCU Development board.

To begin using NodeMCU for IoT applications, we must first understand how to write/download NodeMCU firmware on NodeMCU Development Boards. And before that, where would this NodeMCU firmware be customised to meet our needs?

There are online NodeMCU custom builds available, which allow us to quickly create our own custom NodeMCU firmware.

Refer to getting started with NodeMCU for further information on how to create custom NodeMCU firmware online and download it.

How to write codes for NodeMCU?

After setting up ESP8266 with Node-MCU firmware, let's see the IDE (Integrated Development Environment) required for the development of NodeMCU.

NodeMCU with ESPlorer IDE:

The NodeMCU is usually programmed using Lua scripts. Lua is a lightweight, embeddable scripting language based on the C programming language that is open-source.

Refer to Getting Started with NodeMCU Using ESPlorerIDE for further information on how to build Lua scripts for NodeMCU.

NodeMCU with Arduino IDE:

Another option for building NodeMCU is to use the Arduino IDE, which is a well-known IDE. We can also use the Arduino programming environment to create NodeMCU applications. This makes learning a new language and IDE for NodeMCU much easier for Arduino developers.

Getting started with NodeMCU using ArduinoIDE has more information on how to develop Arduino sketches for NodeMCU.

IV

Implementation of IoT with Raspberry Pi

Raspberry pi:

Raspberry pi is the name of the "credit card-sized computer board" developed by the Raspberry pi foundation, based in the U.K. It gets plugged into a TV or monitor and provides a fully functional computer capability.

It is aimed at imparting knowledge about computing to even younger students at the cheapest possible price.

Although it is aimed at teaching computing to kids, can be used by everyone willing to learn to program, the basics of computing, and build different projects by utilizing its versatility.

Raspberry Pi

Specs of the Computer: –The computer is equipped with a quad-core ARM processor that does not support the same instructions as an X86 desktop processor. It contains 1GB of RAM, four USB ports, one Ethernet connector, a Micro SD slot for storage, one 3.5mm audio/video port, and a Bluetooth connection.

It has got a series of input and output pins that are used for making projects like – home security cameras, Encrypted Door locks, etc.

Versatility of Raspberry Pi: –It is a versatile computer that can be used by individuals of all ages. It can be used to watch videos on YouTube, watch movies, and write in languages such as Python and Scratch, among other things.

As previously said, it contains a variety of I/O pins that allow it to interact with its surroundings, allowing it to be used to create some truly unique and interactive projects.

Examples of the project: – By adding some equipment to it, it may be made into a weather station that can measure temperature, wind speed, humidity, and other variables.

Because of its modest size, it may be used as a home surveillance system; simply add some cameras and you'll have a secure network.

If you enjoy reading books, this gadget can be used as a storage device for thousands of eBooks, as well as a means of accessing them via the internet.

Advantages of Raspberry Pi:

1. Small in Size
2. Open source
3. Low cost
4. USB 3.0 and USB type C power supply
5. More ports

Disadvantages of Raspberry Pi:

1. Unable to complex/Multitasking
2. cannot runX86 OS
3. Low Processor
4. Heat issues (eg. Overheating)

Raspberry pi Board:

Model A Raspberry Pi Board:

The Raspberry Pi board is a Broadcom(BCM2835) SOC(system on chip) board. It comes equipped with an ARM1176JZF-S core CPU, 256 MB of SDRAM and 700 MHz,. The raspberry pi USB 2.0 ports use only external data connectivity options. The board draws its power from a micro USB adapter, with min range of 2. Watts (500 MA). The graphics, specialized chip is designed to speed up the operation of image calculations. This is in built with Broadcom video core IV cable, that is useful if you want to run a game and video through your raspberry pi.

Features of Raspberry PI Model A:

- The Model A raspberry pi features mainly includes
- 256 MB SDRAM memory
- Single 2.0 USB connector
- Dual Core Video Core IV Multimedia coprocessor
- HDMI (rev 1.3 & 1.4) Composite RCA (PAL and NTSC) Video Out
- 3.5 MM Jack, HDMI, Audio Out
- SD, MMC, SDIO Card slot on board storage
- Linux Operating system
- Broadcom BCM2835 SoC full HD multimedia processor
- 8.6cm*5.4cm*1.5cm dimensions

Model B Raspberry pi Board:

The Raspberry Pi is a Broadcom BCM2835 SOC (system on chip board). It comes equipped with a 700 MHz, 512 MB of SDRAM and ARM1176JZF-S core CPU. The USB 2.0 port of the raspberry pi boars uses only external data connectivity options. The Ethernet in the raspberry pi is the main gateway to interconnect with other devices and the internet in model B. This draws its power from a micro USB adapter, with a minimum range of 2.5 watts(500 MA). The graphics, specialized chip is designed to speed up the manipulation of image calculations. This is in built with Broadcom video core IV cable, that is useful if you want to run a game and video through your raspberry pi.

Features of Raspberry PI Model B:

- 512 MB SDRAM memory
- Broadcom BCM2835 SoC full high definition multimedia processor
- Dual-Core Video Core IV Multimedia coprocessor
- Single 2.0 USB connector
- HDMI (rev 1.3 and 1.4) Composite RCA (PAL & NTSC) Video Out
- 3.5 MM Jack, HDMI Audio Out
- MMC, SD, SDIO Card slot on board storage
- Linux Operating system
- Dimensions are 8.6cm*5.4cm*1.7cm
- On board 10/100 Ethernet RJ45 jack

Linux on Raspberry Pi:

The Raspberry Pi's most popular operating system is Linux. To use an OS, we must first construct a Secure Digital (SD) or MicroSD card that contains the OS. A computer with an internet connection and the ability to write to SD or MicroSD cards is required to set up the SD or MicroSD.

Structure Linux on Raspberry Pi:

An operating system is a collection of software, each designed for a specific function.

Linux OS has following components:

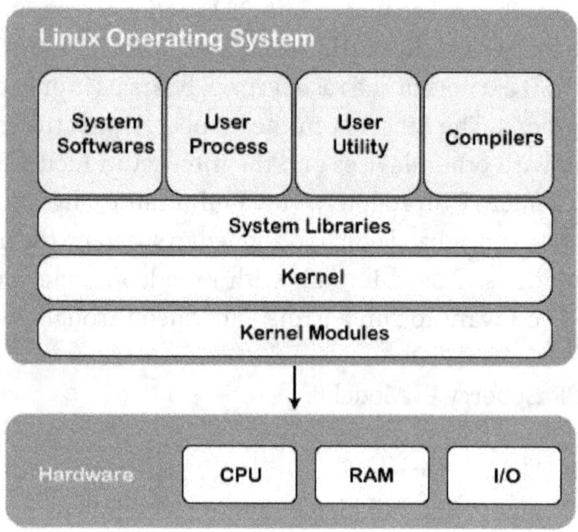

1. Kernel: Linux kernel is the core part of the operating system. It establishes communication between devices and software.

2. System Libraries: System libraries are specialised applications that aid in the use of kernel functionality. To complete a task, a kernel must be triggered, and this triggering is handled by the apps. However, because each kernel has its own set of system calls, programmes must understand how to use them. To connect with the kernel, programmers have created a standard library of operations..

3. System Tools:The Linux operating system comes with a range of utility tools, which are often basic commands. It is a piece of software that the GNU project has produced and released under an open source licence, making it freely available to anyone at all.

4. Development Tools: Your operating system is up and running with the three components listed above. However, you have extra tools and libraries to upgrade your system. Toolchain refers to the set of supplementary tools and libraries created by programmers. A toolchain is a crucial development tool that developers utilise to create a functional application.

5. End User Tools: These finishing tools distinguish a system for a user. Although end tools are not required by the operating system, they are

required by the user.

Why use Linux?: This is one of the most frequently asked questions regarding Linux. Why do we adopt a different, more complicated operating system when we already have a basic one like Windows? As a result, Linuxsystems have a number of characteristics that distinguish it as one of the most widely used operating systems. If you want to get rid of viruses, spyware, slowdowns, crashes, expensive maintenance, and other issues, Linux may be the best operating system for you.

- Free & Open Source Operating System
- It is secure
- Favorable choice of Developers
- A flexible operating system

NOOBS Software: NOOBS stands for "new out-of-the-box software," and it is the simplest method to get started with the Raspberry Pi. NOOBS is simple to copy to your SD or MicroSD card. It gives us a basic menu for installing various operating systems once it has been duplicated.

Although you can buy a card with NOOBS already installed, knowing how to make your own NOOBS cards is always useful.

Download NOOBS Follow the below given steps to download NOOBS –

Step 1 – Go to the website www.raspberrypi.org/downloads/noobs

Step 2 – Select from the two versions of NOOBS available. Version 1 is the main version and includes Raspbian. This is the officially supported OS, which you can use even without any network connection.

Another alternative is to select the operating system from the menu. If you have a network connection, you can download and install the OS from the menu. For your first OS, it's always a good idea to download NOOBS.

MicroSD card Formatting: We must first format our SD or MicroSD card before downloading and installing the operating system. We can use the SD Association's SD card Formatter application tool. The latest version is SD Memory Card Formatter 5.0.1.

Using windows:

Step 1 – Download and install the SD formatter application. It will be as follows

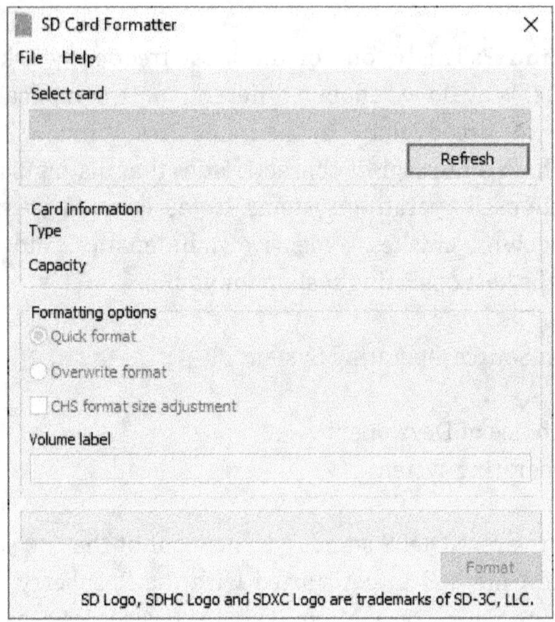

Step 2 – Next, we need to select the drive in which we have our SD High Capacity SDHC/SDXC card. Once selected, click on the format button to format it. The following screen will appear –

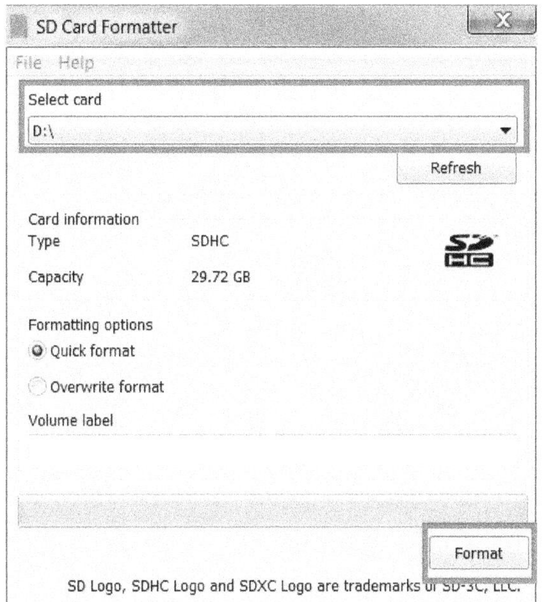

Step 3 – The program will ask for confirmation. You need to click yes to confirm the format process.

Step 4 – Once the format process is completed, your SD card will be formatted completely.

Using Mac OS: The process of formatting is similar to what we did in windows. You just need to download and install the Mac version of SD card formatter.

Using Linux: We will be using the GPartedapplication program, which is an open-source partition manager for Linux.

Use the steps given below to format an SD card in Ubuntu software –

Step 1 – Download and install the GParted application by using the terminal as follows –

sudo apt-get install gparted

Step 2 – Once installation is completed, you need to insert the SD card. Next, by using Unity dash, launch the GParted application.

Step 3 – You will get the screen as below, which shows the partitions of the removable disk. But before starting the formatting, we need to unmount the disk by right-clicking on the partition as shown below –

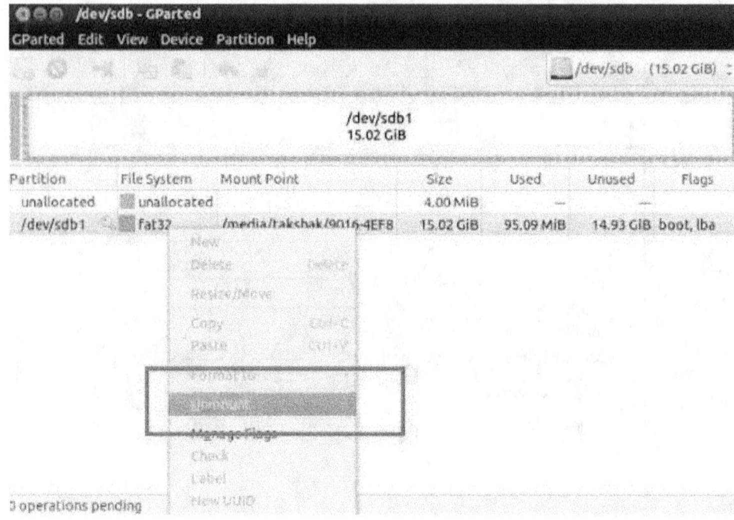

Step 4 – After unmounting, we need to right click on it, which will show us the Format to option. Now from the list, you can choose whatever type of file system you want on the disk. After selecting the drive to format, you need to click on the Tick sign as shown below –

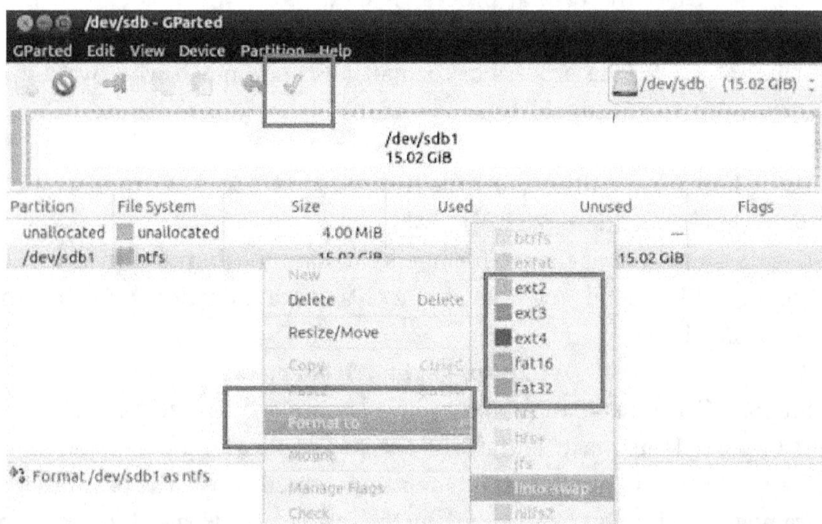

Step 5 – It will show you a couple of warnings and the format procedure will be started.

Install NOOBS to Memory card: You now have a formatted card as well as the.zip file from the Raspberry Pi website. As a result, you can put NOOBS on your card.

Simply double-click the.zip file on a Windows PC. The file will be opened. You may then choose all of the files and copy them to your formatted card once it's opened.

Similarly, double-clicking on the NOOBS.zip file on a Mac OS will reveal the folder containing all of the files. Now, go to the Edit menu and pick "all" from the drop-down menu. Drag and drop all of your files onto your SD card.

In the same way, on Linux we can use the desktop environment to copy the NOOBS .zip files to our SD card.

Flashing a MicroSD card: Some operating systems (OS) aren't supported by NOOBS. The Reduced Instruction Set Computer (RISC) OS is one of them.

To make a card for such an operating system, we must first download it as an image file. After downloading an image file, we must perform the flashing your card procedure. Later on, we can transform the single file into all of the files we require for our card (SD or MicroSD).

Interfacing Raspberry Pi with IoT Services :

Because it includes a quad-core ARM Cortex A7 CPU running at 900 MHz and 1 GB LPDDR2 SDRAM, the Raspberry Pi can serve as an internet gateway. It can be configured to act as an Internet Gateway Device. An IoT project can be made considerably easier by combining an RPi with various off-the-shelf sensors. Many imaginative minds around the world use Raspberry Pi for constructing IoT projects since it requires a microcontroller to process data, Wi-Fi integration to send data to the cloud, and actuators to regulate operations.

Ubuntu Raspberry Pi Generations and Series :

There are three Raspberry Pi series, each of which has multiple generations. Raspberry Pi SBCs have a Broadcom system on a chip (also known as SoC) with a designed ARM-compatible on-chip graphics processing unit and CPU, whilst the Pico version has an RP2040 system on a chip with a developed ARM-compatible CPU.

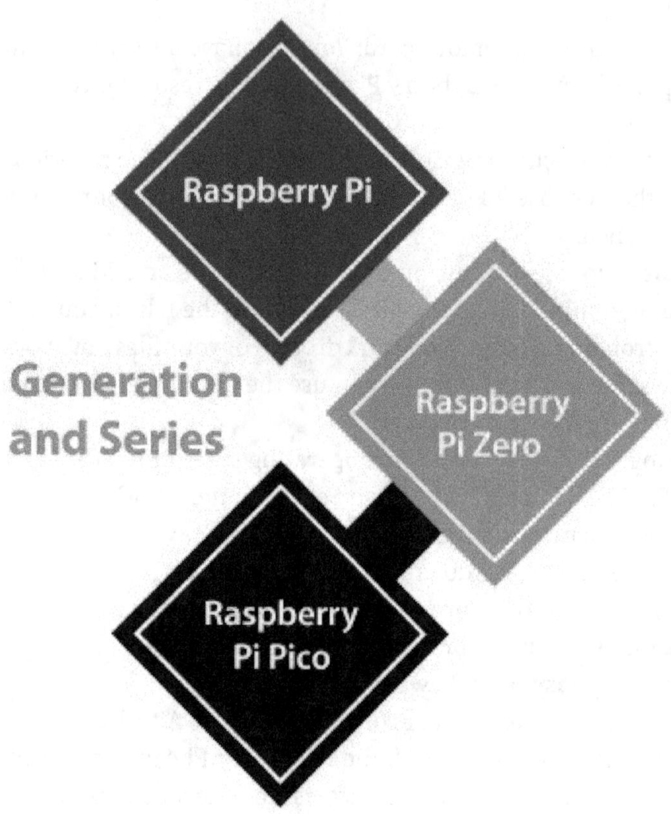

Ubuntu Raspberry Pi Generations and Series

Raspberry Pi:

The Raspberry Pi Model B (first generation) was released in February 2012, followed by the Model A, which was cheaper and simpler. In 2014, the Foundation released a board with a developed structure called Raspberry Pi Model B+. These first-generation boards have ARM11 processors and are roughly the size of a credit card. They reflect the classic mainline form factor. A year later, the developed A+ and B+ models were published. The "Computer Model" for embedded applications was released in April 2014.

The second version of Raspberry Pi 2 was published in 2015 February and initially offered a 900 MHz 32-bit quad-core processor, i.e., ARM Cortex-A7 with 1GB of RAM.

The third version of Raspberry Pi Model B was published in 2016 February with a 64-bit 1.2 GHz quad-core processor, i.e., ARM Cortex-A53, onboard 802.11n WiFi, USB boot, and Bluetooth capabilities.

In celebration of Pi Day 2018, the Raspberry Pi 3 B+ model was announced featuring a faster processor (1.4 GHz), three-times faster 2.4/5 GHz dual-band 802.11ac WiFi, and gigabit Ethernet. Network boot, USB boot, and Power over Ethernet are some of the other features.

The Raspberry Pi 4 Model B was released in June 2019 and features a 64-bit 1.5 GHz ARM Cortex-A72 processor, integrated 802.11ac WiFi, gigabit Ethernet, Bluetooth 5, two USB 3.0 ports, two USB 2.0 ports, 2-8 GB RAM, and support for up to 4000 resolution through mini HDMI connectors pair.

The Raspberry Pi 400 was released in November of 2020. It provides a custom board that is based on the Raspberry Pi 4 and has been redesigned to include a keyboard.

Raspberry Pi Zero:

In November of 2015, the Raspberry Pi Zero was released, with reduced I/O, space, and GPIO (general-purpose input/output) capabilities.

On February 28, 2017, the Raspberry Pi Zero W, a variant of the Zero with Bluetooth and WiFi, was introduced.

On January 12, 2018, the Raspberry Pi Zero WH version was launched, as was the Zero W version with pre-soldered GPIO headers.

On October 28, 2021, Raspberry Pi released the Raspberry Pi Zero 2 W, a Zero W version with a SiP (System in a Package) based on the Raspberry Pi 3 and produced by Raspberry Pi. In comparison to prior versions, the Pi 2 W is competent.

Raspberry Pi Pico:

Raspberry Pi Pico was released in January 2021 for $4. It was the original Raspberry Pi board, and it was based on a single RP2040 microcontroller microprocessor built by Raspberry Pi in the UK. This model has 264GB of RAM and 2MB of flash memory. RUST, C CircuitPython, and MicroPython can all be used to programme it.

It has also teamed up with SparkFun, Arduino, Pimoroni, Adafruit, and Vilros to create accessories for Pico and a variety of other boards based on the RP2040 Silicon Platform. Rather than serving as a general-purpose computer, it is designed for physical computing, similar to how an Arduino works.

Processor:

A Broadcom BCM2835 SoC applied in the initial generation Raspberry Pi contains a 700 GHz processor, i.e., ARM1176JZF-S, RAM, and VideoCore IV Graphics Processing Unit.

It includes level 1 of 16 KB cache and a label 2 of 128 KB cache. The cache of level 2 is primarily used by a GPU. The ARM1176JZF-S is a similar CPU used within the original iPhone, however at the higher clock rate and coordinated with a much faster GPU.

RAM:

The Raspberry Pi 2 includes 1GB RAM.

The Raspberry Pi 3 includes 1GB RAM within the models, i.e., B and B+, and 512 MB RAM within the model, i.e., A+.

The Raspberry Pi Zero W and Zero include 512 MB of RAM.

The Raspberry Pi 4 is present with 8, 4, and 2 GB RAM. Originally, the 1 GB model was present at the launch in 2019 June but it was discontinued in 2020 March, and the 8 GB model was launched in 2020 May.

Networking:

The Model Pi Zero, A+, and A do not contain Ethernet circuitry and they are commonly linked to a network with an independent user-supplied WiFi adapter and USB Ethernet. The Ethernet port is given by a USB Ethernet adaptor (built-in) with the SMSC LAN9514 chip on the B and B+ Models.

The Raspberry Pi Zero W and 3 are equipped with a 2.4 GHz 802.11n WiFi and 4.1 Bluetooth based on a Broadcom chip, i.e., BCM43438 FullMAC along with no official monitor mode support and the Pi 3 version includes a 100/10 Mbit/s Ethernet port as well.

Operating systems:

Raspberry Pi OS is made possible by the Raspberry Pi foundation (also known as Raspbian). It includes third-party Windows 10 IoT Core, Ubuntu, LibreELEC, RISC OS, and specialised distros for classroom administration and Kodi media centre, as well as a 32-bit Debian-based Linux distribution for installation.

Scratch and Python are promoted as the core programming languages, with support for a variety of others. The Raspberry Pi can also run a variety of alternative operating systems. There are a variety of methods for installing multiple operating systems on a single SD card.

Operating system (Linux-based)

Android Things- An Android operating system's embedded version developed for IoT device developed.

Alpine Linux- A distribution of Linux based on BusyBox and musl, "developed for power users who encourage resource efficiency, simplicity, and security.

Arch Linux ARM- An Arch Linux port for ARM processor

Ark OS- Developed for email and website self-hosting

Betocera- Emulation Station for RetroArch and several other emulators is used, along with auxiliary scripts, on a Linus OS (buildroot based). Instead of a traditional Linux distribution with several package managers managing a single software update, Betocera is designed to behave more like the firmware of a video game console, with every emulator and utility updated and included as one package at the time of software updates.

Data Handling Analytics:

The application of data analysis techniques and procedures to gain value from the massive volumes of data created by connected Internet of Things devices is known as IoT analytics. IoT analytics' potential is frequently mentioned in regard to Industrial IoT.

Data analysts add value to their organisations by collecting data on certain issues, interpreting, analysing, and presenting findings in thorough reports." IoT data analysts provide valuable data entry services that enable a company to combine the potential of IoT with excellent data analytics.

The three main classes of IoT analytics: predictive analytics, real-time analytics and descriptive analytics.

Benefits: One of the areas that IoT data analytics can help your business is by improving productivity. By installing smart sensors and devices throughout your facilities, you are able to collect employee engagement data, performance ratings, and many other work-related parameters.

The IoT Analytics Platform module focuses on generating demonstrable business value for M2M/IoT businesses by utilising sophisticated big data processing and real-time data analytics. It delivers detailed information on how clients are interacting with your IoT products.

The real-time nature of IoT data is the key problem. By 2025, 30% of all data will be real-time, with the Internet of Things accounting for roughly 95% of that, 20% of all data will be critical, and 10% of all data will be hypercritical. For businesses to benefit from this type of data, real-time analytics will be required.

V

Ethics and Challenges in IoT

Characterizing the IoT:

Connectivity – The Internet of Things infrastructure relies heavily on connectivity. The Internet of Things (IoT) infrastructure should be connected to the IoT devices. Anyone, wherever, at any time should be able to connect, and this should be ensured at all times. Connection between people via internet devices such as mobile phones and other gadgets, as well as between Internet devices such as routers, gateways, sensors, and so on.

Intelligence and Identity – It is critical to extract knowledge from the generated data. A sensor, for example, creates data, but that data is only useful if it is properly understood. Every IoT gadget has its own identification. This identification is helpful in tracking the equipment and at times for querying its status.

Scalability – Every day, the number of items connected to the IoT zone grows. As a result, an IoT setup should be able to handle the tremendous growth. The data generated as an outcome is enormous, and it should be handled appropriately.

Dynamic and Self-Adapting (Complexity) –IoT devices should be able to adapt to changing settings and circumstances on the go. Assume you have a surveillance camera. It should be able to work in a variety of settings and lighting scenarios (morning, afternoon, night).

Architecture – In nature, IoT architecture cannot be homogeneous. It should be hybrid, allowing items from many manufacturers to work together in an IoT network. The Internet of Things (IoT) is not held by any engineering branch. When many domains join together, IoT becomes a reality.

Safety – When all of a user's gadgets are connected to the internet, there is a risk that his or her sensitive personal information will be compromised. The user may suffer a loss as a result of this. As a result, data security is a key concern. Aside from that, the equipment required is massive. IoT networks may be at risk as well. As a result, equipment safety is crucial.

IoT security and privacy concerns:

Although IoT is rapidly growing, it still faces security and privacy issues:

Security Risks: Your PC or laptop is connected to Internet of Things (IoT) devices. Because of the lack of protection, your personal information may be leaked while the data is being collected and communicated to the IoT device. A consumer network is used to link IoT devices. Other systems are also connected to this network. So if the IoT device contains any security vulnerabilities, it can be harmful to the consumer's network. This vulnerability can attack other systems and damage them. Sometimes unauthorized people might exploit the security vulnerabilities to create risks to physical safety.

Privacy Risks: In IoT, Because devices are interconnected with a variety of hardware and software, there is a high risk of sensitive data being exposed as a result of illegal tampering. All of the devices communicate personal information such as the user's name, address, date of birth, health card information, credit card information, and much more without encryption. Though there are worries about security and privacy, IoT brings value to our lives by allowing us to manage our everyday routine tasks remotely and automatically, and it is a game-changer for industries.

IoT applications across industries: Several organisations are now assisting businesses in utilising IoT to address long-standing, industry-specific difficulties. They create IoT solutions that link things, collect data, and generate insights, all while reducing expenses, improving efficiency, and increasing income.

Trends in IoT:

If we implement IoT, we will increase our society's and economy's digitization by connecting items and people via a connected or communication medium. When it comes to device-to-device contact, IoT allows consumers to have more control over their daily lives through effective monitoring. Let's see the trends in IoT app development areas.

Wearable gadgets: Since the release of smartwatches and smartglasses, wearable gadgets have been a big issue in the tech industry. From fitness trackers to GPS sneakers, there are a plethora of wearable devices on the market today.

Connected Car: This is a relatively new notion that is likely to gain traction gradually. Developing an app for the automobile industry often takes two to four years. Connected car solutions are being developed by everyone from giant automakers to small start-ups. If BMW and Ford do not disclose Internet-connected car solutions soon, Google, Apple, and Microsoft will build and market the next generation of linked car solutions.

Smart Home: IoT provides us with a space where we can relax and conveniently handle our everyday activities in our hectic lives. Smart thermostats, connected lights, smart fridges, smart televisions, smart door locks, and other smart home devices are among the most popular.

Smart City: People can avoid concerns such as traffic management, social security, environmental monitoring, trash management, and water distribution by living in a smart city. Improved IoT apps will aid in the resolution of different traffic, noise, and air pollution issues, as well as making cities safer.

Smart Grid: It's a crucial area of IoT. It delivers automated information about consumers and electrical providers. It always contributes to increased efficiency, economies, and electrical reliability.

Along with these trends, the IoT market is booming with other emerging trends such as smart retail, industrial Internet, connected health, smart supply chain, smart farming, smart energy and so on. With the support of the cloud platform, even artificial intelligence (AI) has the potential to improve IoT.

Robotic Process Automation (RPA) systems, which translate corporate processes into software-driven, rule-based decision trees, rely heavily on IoT. For enterprises, RPA offers cost savings and scalability benefits, as well as faster transaction times for customers.

Disrupting Control Crowdsourcing in IoT: In the field of the Internet of Things, crowdsourcing is paving the way for new types of experiments. It connects existing IoT testbeds to third-party resources, but more crucially, it allows testbeds to leak into the real world and engage with end-users more directly.

Disadvantages of Crowdsourcing: No confidentiality, Poor quality entries, Wrong direction, Popularity misleads, Stolen or recycled names.

Advantages of crowdsourcing include cost savings, speed, and the ability to work with people who have skills that an in-house team may not have.

Physical thing Electronics internet service:

A thing, in the context of the Internet of things (IoT), is an entity or physical object that has a unique identifier, an embedded system and the ability to transfer data over a network. The Internet of Things (IoT) refers to the physical objects that are connected to the Internet and, therefore, to all other physical objects.

IoT Devices and IoT Protocols are part of the physical design of the Internet of Things. Things are node devices with distinct identities that can perform remote sensing, actuation, and monitoring. IoT Protocols facilitate communication between devices and cloud-based servers via the Internet.

Environmental monitoring:

The applications of IoT in environmental monitoring are broad – environmental protection, extreme weather monitoring, water safety, endangered species protection, commercial farming, and more. In these applications, sensors detect and measure every type of environmental change.

4 types of environmental monitoring :

- Air Monitoring.
- Water Monitoring.
- Waste Monitoring.
- Remote Sensing.

Environmental Monitoring Benefits:

- Validation and verification of cleaning and sanitation programs. ...
- Provides data of the overall effectiveness of your sanitary program, personnel practices, and operations procedures. ...
- Provides data about indicator organisms, spoilage organisms, and pathogens to prevent outbreaks.

Example of environmental monitoring: One of the most familiar examples is the monitoring of numbers of Salmonid fish such as brown trout or Atlantic salmon in river systems and lakes to detect slow trends in adverse environmental effects.

The IoT as a part of the solution cautious optimism:

Almost every industry has benefited from Internet of Things (IoT) solutions, which have made it easier to start new businesses and increase productivity. IoT solutions have made it easier to connect devices, manage tasks, analyse opportunities, and securely send data.

The Internet of Things will have a tremendous positive influence on citizens, businesses, and governments, ranging from cutting healthcare expenses and improving quality of life to reducing carbon footprints, increasing access to education in marginalised places, and improving transportation safety.

Major solutions:

- Understanding the exact need of the business and formulating a framework
- Building the tailor-made module
- Operating and maintaining the system